# WITNESSES TO POWER

Lovers of China – in fact, all China-watchers – have marveled at the expansion of the Christian community there in the past twenty years. The authors have penetrated remote areas of the country and remote areas of faith to bring us these stories. At least three facts stand out: large areas of material poverty during a time of economic expansion for much of the country; the suffering and courage of many new believers; the spread of the gospel by individual, often isolated, Christians.

CREIGHTON LACY
Professor Emeritus of World Christianity
The Divinity School, Duke University

The revival of the church in Mainland China is one of the greatest and most moving sagas in church history since Pentecost. We Christians in the West need to be aware of the mighty acts of God in China and the faithfulness of His witnesses in the most populous nation on earth. What we read here will teach us humility, wean us from superficiality, and encourage us in our own Christian pilgrimage.

TONY LAMBERT
Author, *China's Christian Millions*

As the title suggests, *Witnesses to Power* is an account both of God's miraculous work in China and of the believers who have participated in that work. By skillfully weaving their stories together with insightful analysis of the Chinese social and political context, Yamamori and Chan have created a masterful portrait of the church in China today. The picture that emerges is one of God's faithfulnesses, exhibited through the lives of ordinary people who exhibit extraordinary perseverance and creativity in the face of seemingly insurmountable obstacles. As the authors point out, the Chinese church offers much to enrich the spirituality of the church outside China. For those who come to learn, who are willing to 'serve with Chinese Christians as equal partners', there is also much that can be done to encourage the Chinese church as it seeks to witness to God's power in a rapidly changing China.

BRENT FULTON
Editor of *China Source*

This remarkable book will both challenge and inspire you. Ted Yamamori and Kim-kwong Chan have compiled a compelling series of uncommon stories containing first-hand accounts of the extraordinary way that God has been moving in the hearts and lives of many who have decided to follow Jesus in China. You will be touched in heart and mind as you read these unforgettable pages.

PAUL A. CEDAR
Chairman, Mission America
Executive Chair, LCWE

# WITNESSES TO POWER

*Stories of God's Quiet Work
in a Changing China*

Tetsunao Yamamori
and Kim-kwong Chan

paternoster
press

Paternoster Press is an imprint of Paternoster Publishing,
PO Box 300, Carlisle, Cumbria CA3 0QS, UK
and Paternoster Publishing USA
PO Box 1047, Waynesboro, GA 30830–2047
www.paternoster-publishing.com

**British Library Cataloguing in Publication Data**

A catalogue record for this book is available from the British Library

ISBN 1–84227–041–9

Cover design by Campsie
Typeset by Waverley Typesetters, Galashiels
Printed and bound in the USA by
RR Donnelley and Sons, Harrisonburg, VA

# Contents

# Acknowledgments

We wish to acknowledge the contributions of those courageous Christians in China whose inspirational testimonies constitute the bulk of this book. We also thank Dr Alan Hunter for providing us with helpful information used in our 'Introduction'. Above all, we express our gratitude to Stan Guthrie whose expert editorial assistance enabled this book to meet its publication deadline.

# Foreword

The Book *Witnesses to Power: Stories of God's Quiet Work in a Changing China* expresses a paradox in its title. God has been powerfully at work in China, but his power has been so quiet that many Christians in the Western world have little idea of what is happening.

The authors of this intriguing book come from different backgrounds which give their work a perspective not found in other books on China. Tetsunao Yamamori is President of Food for the Hungry International and, in his travels and books, has focused on the economically most needy in the world. Kim-kwong Chan is an ordained minister with theological training and currently serves as Executive Secretary for Education and Training of Hong Kong Christian Council. Both are also engaged as visiting professors in two prestigious Chinese universities.

If I were to use single words to characterize this work, they would be breadth, diversity, balance, and challenge. The stories, which comprise a major portion of the book, extend to China's far northwest in Xinjiang province to Fujian along the southern coast of the country. The ministries recorded embrace not only rural and urban evangelism, but also healing and exorcism, compassionate care for needy children, community life of the Jesus family, church planting and growth in remote areas not penetrated by an outside Christian witness, and the impact of the gospel to produce economic prosperity and reduce crime. The breadth of the book is also seen from the timing of the stories – some going back to the Boxer tragedy in China and others brought right up to the present. Church growth has produced huge congregations in some areas, and yet there are also tales of persecution, imprisonment, and cruelty.

Another commendable feature of this book is the diversity of the people and situations related in the stories. Some of the accounts are about Han Christians and Han society. Others describe God's work in Lahu villages along the Burma border or among Lisu, Nus, and Dulong peoples in the nearly inaccessible Dulong valley in far northwest Yunnan. Resources for the stories come from participants, from close observers, and from government sources. In several instances, Dr Chan himself is personally involved, which gives even further credibility to the stories. The Christian workers involved are young and old, men and women.

As most Westerners seek to understand what God is doing in China, the big lack is balance. They polarize between churches related to the China Christian Council and the autonomous, often non-registered, church congregations. Some wish to see the renewal of the pre-1949 Western missionary movement or they believe there is no longer need in China for outside help. Yamamori and Chan do not ignore these tensions, neither do they polarize. In their extensive introduction, in the more concise statement accompanying each story, and particularly in their conclusion, they present both sides of these issues. They even give an overview of recent dissension between adminis-tration and some students at Jinling Union Theological

Seminary in Nanjing. God has his people in many different groups in China. He has done a tremendous work in China without outside missionaries and yet there may be some areas where, with consultation and cooperation, outside help might be welcomed.

Reading this book is a challenge to faith, endurance, and action. The men and women involved in these stories are models of how God's people should serve him in difficult situations. Most of us in the Western world will not have such experiences, but we can learn from these dedicated servants. Even as we ponder about appropriate ways to work together with and help the churches in China, we must never forget that they have more to teach us than we have to teach them.

In addition to the twelve stories which form the core of the book, the authors also include a detailed analysis of the Lisu society, largely Christian, and the integration of faith and culture. This presentation, in addition to the stories, leads them to advocate that the best way for outside groups to be involved in China will be in the use of 'unconventional mission methods'. These will include holistic ministries helping churches both to evangelize and to seek the economic well-being of Christians and the societies, both Han and minority, in which they live.

Yamamori and Chan are to be congratulated for a superb book which paints a well-rounded picture of how God is working in a quiet and powerful way in China's huge nation.

Ralph Covell
*Senior Professor of World Christianity*
*Denver Seminary*

# Introduction

After several decades of silence, the church in China re-emerged in the 1980s as the fastest-growing Christian community in contemporary times – from an estimated three million to at least twenty-five million. While China is the largest political entity with an antireligious ideology, Christians in China demonstrate an amazing ability to spread their faith.

How has this happened? Perhaps the stories in this volume about the living faith of many ordinary Chinese Christians can provide us with some answers. We have collected testimonies of the faith journeys of Chinese Christians, who are unknown, ordinary people, with extraordinary stories to tell. They come from different regions in China, from the grasslands in the northwest to the mountainous areas of the southwest. Some are highly educated professionals, while others are farmers who can barely write their names. Speaking different languages, they are members of different minority groups. Some are from officially sanctioned Christian groups, others from the unregistered Christian groups. Yet they are united in that – like leaven – they continue to silently build and sustain the church in China.

Despite 30 years of severe repression, the church in China grew rapidly after 1949. Distressed, Chinese Communist

Party (CCP) officials referred to this as 'Christianity Fever'. The church apparently had a second growth spurt in the mid-1990s, with much of it occurring in rural areas.

In November 1995, the Public Security Bureau (PSB) issued an internal statement telling all branches of the state to increase their control over Protestants, noting that they numbered twenty-five million. The PSB was concerned that many young people were joining the church, while the numbers joining the CCP were falling, especially in rural areas. Moreover, increasing numbers of Party members were withdrawing due to religious conversion. In 1996, even faculty members of the CCP Central Academy had converted to Christianity and were influencing students before being arrested.

Apart from the spiritual vitality of believers and the powerful working of the Holy Spirit, the following are among the most important factors in the growth of the Chinese church:

1  Christianity is seen as, in some sense, an improvement on traditional Chinese beliefs: it offers prayer, healing, fellowship, a moral code, a rationale for suffering and the promise of salvation. It is wider in scope, more universal and less tied to traditional society than folk religion.

2  Christianity has a highly flexible and successful organizational form. Christian groups range from family prayer meetings to village communities addressed by itinerant preachers, from sophisticated underground networks to the powerful and efficient national organization.

3  The church benefited in the 1980s and 1990s from the prestige of the West, as a symbol of a material

and political system that many felt was superior to their own.

4 Many believers were brought up in families or communities that had been Christian for some time. Especially in the southeast of China and in cities like Shanghai, present communities are descendants or extensions of previous ones.

5 A key strength of Protestantism has been its evangelistic nature, in particular a strong oral culture focused on preaching and accounts of healing and miracles.

6 Christianity offers attractive forms of worship, which are times of emotional release and spiritual enrichment.

7 It offers self-respect and enhanced personal identity. The affirmation of selfhood and individuality is much appreciated in a society which has been oppressed for many decades.

8 Young people, and especially women, can exercise their talents as leaders, scholars, musicians, or organizers in church groups. For all who are excluded from the political and civil power structure, religion can offer an alternative, productive outlet for their energies.

9 Young people, especially in rural areas, need a sense of mission in life, and evangelism is a viable option. Itinerant preachers, many of whom are teenagers, travel widely, hosted by local Christian groups, and feel themselves called by God. There is a curious parallel between their messianic excursions and those of the Red Guards who spread the word of Mao in the 1960s during the cultural revolution.

10 In this context, the eschatological tone of many Christian communities is very attractive to poorer peasants, whose life may often be harsher than before the economic reforms. These people look forward to the end time.

11 It is cheaper to worship as a Christian than to participate in folk religion. Folk religion demands high spending on materials such as incense and paper money.

We will probably never know when underground Christian practice and evangelism became so powerful after the churches were closed in the late 1950s. Some reports suggest that it was during the chaotic years of the cultural revolution. There were several contributing factors. Former Red Guards became disillusioned with politics and turned to religion in the late 1970s. Also, many believers had been sent to labor camps or remote rural areas; after their release, some had attained great sympathy and reputation among local Christians. Further, overseas Chinese Christians brought in Bibles and other literature, and gospel radio also left a mark.

We should remember that current relations between the Chinese state and religious communities are the product of a long historical process. The Chinese state has actually exerted control over religious groups at least since the Tang dynasty. The concepts of separation of church and state and of religious freedom, while familiar to Westerners, are alien to Chinese believers. Christians in China will create their own unique model of church–state relations.

In 1979, the Three-Self Patriotic Movement (TSPM) was reconstituted after its suspension during the cultural revolution, and soon afterwards a related organization called the China Christian Council (CCC) was formed.

These two organizations, known as the *lianghui* ('two committees'), form the state-sanctioned leadership of the Protestant community. Their functions are not clearly delineated, and many leading figures hold positions in both organizations, such as K.H. Ting (Ding Guangxun), Bishop of Nanjing, who is honorary president of both.

Power resides in the standing committees, which oversee church policy, relations with overseas churches, pastoral affairs, and personnel appointments. Most members of the national standing committees are also leaders of provincial or municipal Protestant organizations, which effectively supervise local church affairs. These leaders are nominally elected by the church members themselves but in practice they are usually Party nominees.

This naturally leads to some resentment among Christian groups, who feel they are under constant surveillance, and that the church is run by non-Christians. The level of supervision is much higher in urban than in rural areas, however. The original purposes of the TSPM were to eliminate foreign influence, to unite Protestants in one organization, and to promote CCP policies inside the church. These remain part of their charter. However, in the 1980s and 1990s, as the Protestant communities grew stronger, the 'two committees' also legitimized and promoted the religion. The official leaders have negotiated the return of church property, the right to print Bibles and other literature, and the opening of seminaries and thousands of churches and meeting points. Bishop Ting and others have advocated religious freedom.

The TSPM is not a monolithic entity, but a loose fellowship with diverse views. Many younger pastors (and some older ones) are rebellious and may refuse to accept their leadership's claim to speak for the Protestant community in China. Thus, it is wrong to regard the TSPM and all those connected with it as puppet organizations. (For more on dissent in the official church, see Appendix 1.)

The other major institutional element of Chinese Protestantism is the so-called 'house church' movement. China has a long tradition of Christian home meetings, especially in rural areas. Christianity has often been introduced to a village by one or two families, and it might take several generations before a church could be built. In the cities, it has been common for families to hold prayer meetings for themselves, and perhaps their extended family, in the privacy of their homes.

During the years of repression, the faith survived in this organizational form and the home meetings indeed appear to have spread their influence during the 1960s and 1970s. In the 1980s, home meetings and house churches expanded far beyond their original scope. Some developed extensive national and international networks, with thousands of members. Some even had publishing and training facilities. To reflect this change, some say that the term 'autonomous Christian communities' (ACCs) is a more appropriate term than 'house churches' for this group.

The doctrines and ecclesiology of the ACCs are diverse. Many have inherited their practices from groups that were formed in the 1920s. Interaction with popular culture has sometimes led to syncretism with local cults, and in some areas a Pentecostal style of worship has been practiced since around 1910. Speaking in tongues and faith healing are widespread and influential, but many groups, on the contrary, are pietistic. For example, most 'little flock' congregations oppose charismatic styles of worship and place emphasis on literal belief in the Bible, and on what they assert are apostolic traditions.

Energetic and well-financed evangelical Chinese ministries, usually based in Hong Kong or the US, have provided training materials, personnel, and successful radio stations that reach across China. Meanwhile, many ACCs emphasize martyrdom and a radical missionary orientation. Asceticism and a self-sacrificing life for the gospel are popular. The highest ideal for believers is to abandon everything to follow Christ. Such calls appear to succeed in arousing religious zeal among young converts, especially in rural areas.

The extent of Christian activity outside TSPM supervision has aroused considerable controversy. Government sources tend to claim that the movement hardly exists, while many groups abroad seem to view the movement through a romantic haze. In fact, it is extremely difficult to gather reliable information about the ACCs as they are spread through the countryside. They publish little and most receive few visitors.

From 1992 to 1996, China experienced rapid economic growth and a significant shift in social values. Individual competitiveness and acquisitiveness were stimulated, and China entered a phase reminiscent of Taiwan and Hong Kong in the 1950s: a feeling that anyone can become a millionaire overnight. But the veneer of rampant consumerism has disguised China's central problems: overpopulation, low productivity, and serious weaknesses in infrastructure. While some have prospered, the vast majority suffer from high inflation and loss of security. There is also tremendous resentment at government corruption. Hostility to inflation, social polarization and corruption sparked the protests of 1989.

While Deng Xiaoping and his clique pushed on with economic reforms, they were by no means so liberal in the political sphere. The Party issued regulations between 1990 and 1995 to tighten controls on religious groups. These decrees, and the overall trend of religious policy, are consistent: On the one hand, the government confirms that religion is basically legal and tolerated; on the other, it asserts its right to exercise strict supervision and control.

For many years, government officials have promised that China will enact a comprehensive new law on religious affairs, and several academic institutions have formulated draft documents. While the government is by no means happy with the current state of religion, it will continue to use the administrative apparatus and procedures already in place. However, there are also signs of the government not only supervising religious groups, but dictating their practices and doctrines. For example, faith healing and exorcism are forbidden, since they allegedly promote a superstitious worldview and undermine faith in science. Likewise, pastors are strongly discouraged from preaching on the Second Coming or the Day of Judgment, doctrines that the Party finds hard to stomach.

If the official line on religion seems relatively stable, local implementation of policies is more worrying. Seeing their colleagues in other departments reap rich rewards, there are great temptations for Religious Affairs Bureau (RAB) cadres to squeeze money from religious believers, who are in a relatively vulnerable position.

The reintegration of Hong Kong into China may have several important consequences. The estimated quarter of a million Hong Kong Christians are often well-educated, dedicated, articulate, vocal and socially active, with a wide background of church life and social service. Many of them have actively supported churches and Christian groups in China, taking in literature and training materials, facilitating networking, overseas study, the exchange of information and so on.

On the other hand, there may be acute short-term problems. Hong Kong Christians are under increasing pressure to conform to dictates from PRC (People's Republic of

China) officials, inside and outside church circles. The authorities keep close watch on the minutiae of church affairs. If all church groups maintain self-censorship in line with official policy, Beijing would probably prefer to avoid a crackdown in Hong Kong because of the inevitable international outcry. However, it might eventually implement one anyway if, for example, the church refused to maintain silence on human rights issues.

Many international denominations are already quietly withdrawing funds and personnel from the territory, and many elderly pastors, with memories of earlier persecution, are also leaving. This creates an additional burden of fatigue and low morale for those who remain.

On the other hand, some groups, particularly those with a strong missionary impulse, are establishing new bases in Hong Kong with a view to increasing their 'penetration' of China. Quite possibly China will consider this an abuse of Hong Kong's special status and may use such alleged 'anti-China' activities as a pretext for a crackdown on the Hong Kong church as a whole.

How does the Chinese church conduct its international affairs, and how do overseas churches relate to China? The official church leaders in the TSPM and the CCC are very keen to maintain good relations with churches around the world. There is a constant stream of visitors, ranging from pastors to archbishops. The high point was the admittance of the CCC into the World Council of Churches in 1991. These contacts have generally been beneficial to the Chinese church and have led to concrete results, such as scholarships to Western seminaries and universities and, perhaps most important, the establishment of a very successful printing press for Bibles in Nanjing.

ACCs, on the other hand, have had much contact with individuals and groups who enter China without official permission, most of them overseas Chinese evangelicals, often with family members and connections inside China. Since the late 1970s, they have taken in Bibles and other literature, conducted training courses, provided information and money, and helped in numerous ways. In return, visitors often feel immensely privileged to witness the growth of religion in such difficult circumstances. A frequent comment is that the sense of spirituality is far deeper in the poverty of China than in the wealth of Hong Kong or California.

Christians from outside China who are interested in working with the Chinese church have various options. The most straightforward is to correspond formally with the official church and its representatives, for example, the Amity Foundation in Hong Kong. Contacting the autonomous communities is more dangerous. Apart from friendly contacts, dialogue and sharing of faith, some organizations have set up ambitious programs that would be interpreted by the authorities as 'ideological penetration' at best, such as Bible smuggling, large financial donations for evangelism and so on.

In the 1990s, a new international factor influenced church development in China, namely, support from Korea. Christian groups from South Korea have been making large contributions to the ethnically Korean Christian communities in northeast China. The RAB, the TSPM and city governments have repeatedly called for vigilance against this foreign infiltration, and it is true that the donations are causing some tension: church communities comprising ethnic Koreans are much wealthier than those of ethnic Hans. It is not yet clear how the Chinese authorities will handle relations with Korean Christians.

Chinese church institutions will probably change significantly in the coming years. Inside the TSPM, the old guard will soon be gone. In a recent meeting in Guangdong, the average age of delegates was seventy-four. Bishop Ting himself has recognized that 'leaders at various levels are mostly church people of the 1940s, with some people of the 1950s'.

The real shakeup will come if the Communist Party itself loses power. Of course, the Chinese state has asserted its right to supervise religious groups for centuries, and perhaps no future government will allow complete religious freedom. However, it is unlikely that future governments will want to prop up a church institution perceived by many congregations as a state imposition. It is indeed difficult to foresee how the various Protestant communities – those that have been related to the TSPM, those that have been opposed to it in principle, and those who are in the middle – would renegotiate their relationships.

Many Western Christians have viewed China as a target field for missions. But most Chinese have been converted by other Chinese, not by Westerners. Typically, a handful become Christian during a period of contact with an overseas missionary. From then on, those few do the preaching and church planting. Since 1900, tens of thousands of men and, particularly, women (the so-called Bible-women) have worked as itinerant preachers and unpaid lay workers.

Chinese Protestantism may yet become a force on the world scene. Until now, its influence overseas has been minimal. Perhaps a parallel may be drawn with the Chinese Communist state, which has played an essentially introverted role for the last five decades before beginning to assert itself in recent years. Almost certainly Chinese influence will be felt more widely as China's economic and commercial interests expand, especially in southeast Asia and among overseas Chinese communities throughout the world. It would be surprising if the Chinese church, with its great evangelistic ardor, did not follow suit. Who knows whether, in a few decades, Chinese Christians may feel a call to convert the heathen areas of the West?

# Chapter 1

# A Snow Lotus

*In the late 1940s, many highly educated Chinese Christians from the relatively wealthy coastal areas felt called to spread the gospel in Muslim-dominated Xinjiang, the poorest part of China. The journey to resettle themselves and their families took between three weeks and three months. Bandits and diseases killed many as they rode camels into the desert areas of Xinjiang. After the Communists took over northeast China, almost all of the new migrants were charged as spies. Most received long prison terms; many were executed. Their families suffered discrimination from the larger society for several decades. Yet, despite the extreme hardship, they managed not only to survive but also to spread the gospel throughout this frontier region. These anonymous missionaries established most of the Christian communities in Xinjiang. Gan Ping, a lady evangelist, recounts her life and faith in Xinjiang, a place where believers still face much persecution.*

My mother was a young evangelist who passed away when I was two. I have no memories of her. My only relative in this icy wilderness was my father – a shepherd with a humpback. A highly educated man, he came to northern Xinjiang, bordering Siberia, when I was four. The winter is interminable and extremely cold. Whenever a snowstorm came, we would stay in our hut, burning cow dung to keep warm.

We were poor. My father sewed and resewed patches on my tattered jacket to keep it going. I enjoyed this sense of family. I would lean on my father's back and sing a local folk song: 'The mountain is so high that no grass can grow. The wind is so strong that the stones are running . . .' Like those accustomed to suffering, I did not feel that my life was harsh. People can be happy while living in poverty. A lotus can thrive in the snow. My father taught me maths, Chinese, music, English and the Bible.

When I was very young, I was able to talk with my father in English. Once, when the Red Guards arrested him, he told me in English, 'Hide the Bible in old clothes and put it under the hay.' The zealots did not know English, so they took away all my father's books except the Bible. I still have this Bible. I learned how to survive from my father; most importantly, I learned how to walk the way of the cross.

Another time, the Red Guards locked my father up for five years for 'crimes against the Communist Party and the people'. It took a 16-hour bus ride for me to visit him. My father had studied in the USA and was one of the first geophysical engineers in China. He had given up his comfortable life to come to this frontier area in 1947 and preach the gospel. His background and his unusual choice made him a suspect in the minds of the Communists, who believed him to be a spy working for the 'American imperialists'. My father did not say a word in his own defense during his trial. The guards told me that I had to renounce my relationship with him, but I would not.

Yet in my daily prayers I always asked for things for me, not for my Lord. In times of pain and despair, I even blamed Christ for allowing so much suffering in my family.

Once when I visited my father, the guard was away looking for matches for a smoke. My father told me, 'In times of trial, learn to depend on Jesus.' This made me think. I started to rely on the strength of God to overcome these difficulties. I was fifteen at the time. I felt like a grain of sand washed ashore by waves, yet even a grain of sand reflects the sunshine. I thought that perhaps that is the will of the Creator. I began to really know the Lord when I was living by myself at home.

One cold evening, as the wind was blowing through the window cracks, I woke up from a nightmare. The fire in the stove was extinguished and darkness came through the door cracks. 'What kind of world is it?' I screamed tearfully in the dark. 'Are we born to suffer?' I was ready to jump out of bed and open the door so that the bitter cold could kill me. But a voice suddenly stopped me: 'In times of trial, learn to depend on the Lord.' I collapsed like a leaf falling to the ground. Shaking, I prayed, 'Merciful God, if you want to take me away, let the wind blow open the door. If you want me to remain on earth, don't forsake me.' Then I felt as if something surrounded me. The sound of the wind and the coldness disappeared. The sense of peace I felt is beyond words.

I and other young people who were regarded as intellectuals where I lived were sent down to the collective farms. This was the first time that I tried to share the gospel with others. One day, while we were in the field, I was moved to share the gospel with a young girl who had learned English from me. She showed no response. At that moment, the commissar came and sent her away. I was afraid that she would tell him the whole incident and I would be doomed, just like my father. It seemed as if the others were trying to avoid me that afternoon. I began to harbor the thought that God had deserted me.

I later found out that the girl had been called out because her mother was seriously ill. I felt so ashamed of my paranoia. I had thought I was so strong in my many trials, yet I was so weak. That night, I went to the forest and prayed that God would crush my old self. God showed me that there is only one way to him – total dedication.

Afterward, I kept on praying for that young girl. I asked the Holy Spirit to work in her heart. Twenty days later she returned. Immediately she found me and asked many questions. All I could tell her were my own spiritual experiences. To my surprise, she tearfully accepted Christ as her personal Savior. This was a terrifying choice for her: If anyone knew about her decision, she would lose everything. Soon she was sent to work at a military printing factory, where she kept on sharing the gospel with her friends and neighbors. She still uses the Bible we hand-copied together at night by the light of an oil lamp.

Until this experience, I had not thought about the burden of evangelization. But in sharing my faith I experienced the power of God and a joy that is beyond words. Jesus is the Shepherd. He loves his flock, not just one sheep. I have discovered that when you have the burden to sow the seeds, he has already prepared everything for you.

In 1975, the leaders from the Educational Ministry of Xinjiang Autonomous Region came to our farm to recruit students. They heard that I had studied English by myself and they wanted to admit me to the university. There was a big debate on whether a descendant from the family of the 'reactionary class' should be admitted. I knew, however, that God was leading me to a new place, so I waited with a victorious heart. I was chosen for training.

The first time I set foot in a classroom was the day I entered the university. I knew that because God had led me here, he must have a plan for me. I decided to live out the glory of the Lord even though probably no one knew I was a Christian. I saw myself as a mirror of God to shine forth his holiness, and Christ's moral values guided my conduct.

Very soon I was known as a model student in the English department. Everyone praised my good deeds without knowing where they came from. Because of my good pronunciation of English, the university typed my speeches as teaching materials. I became the pride of the department. Yet it bothered me to conceal my love for the Lord and the Bible. I even had to hide the Bible among my textbooks.

I was the only student who was neither a Party member nor a Communist Youth League member. The university's revolutionary propaganda brigade thought that everything good must be from the Party. Therefore, its members tried to persuade me to join the Communist Youth League so that the whole class would be 'Red'. But how can a Christian join an atheistic organization? I tried to avoid the issue by giving excuses, such as 'I am not good enough', or 'I am not qualified'.

The Communist Youth League organized a series of meetings to 'help' me. I knew that I could no longer hide my real identity. This would shame the name of the Lord. I decided that since everyone was praising my good deeds, it was time to let the glory go to God. The Holy Spirit granted me strength. At one of these 'helping sessions', I told them that I had not joined the League because I was a Christian. This shocked everyone, and the university leaders were infuriated. They wondered how, during the cultural revolutionary era in a revolutionary university, someone with antirevolutionary 'feudal superstition' could get in there.

The university authority ordered me to clarify the root of my faith. Amid all the shouting around me, I closed my eyes and prayed silently: 'I have lived under the protection of my heavenly Father since I was very small. If this is your will to test my loyalty, please grant me the gift of strength in my weakness.' I opened my eyes. The whole place was absolutely silent. In front of more than two hundred students and faculty members, I shared with them my sins, my insignificance before the cross, and the sufferings of Jesus for mankind. I also told them that Jesus would not harm society; rather, he would lead us to discover beauty and eternity.

Most of those at the meeting had only heard of Christianity through Party propaganda. But as they witnessed a Christian standing in front of them, all those attacks on Christianity vanished. In a world full of class struggle and hatred, Christianity looks pure and holy.

As I finished my statement, the revolutionary propaganda brigade suddenly realized that I was using the occasion to spread 'poison'. They demanded that everybody criticize me on the spot. However, people had already felt the goodness of God, and the session was soon terminated.

The first thing that welcomes the light of salvation is persecution. I knew that I had lost the chance for an education in the university. University was important to me but it is nothing compared to God. The grace of God demands that we forsake ourselves. I knew I could leave everything but God.

As I demonstrated my true identity, determined to bear the cross, many who watched me from the darkness were shocked by the light of salvation in my life. I became a celebrity. People talked about me behind my back, usually more sympathetic than sarcastic, more from concern than criticism. Some even dared to ask me questions about salvation in private. I knew that God had prepared a field for me in which to sow seeds. Our students would be sent all over Xinjiang as teachers and translators, and some might carry the gospel all over Xinjiang. But I would soon be expelled from the university.

Still, I knew that if God wants us to finish a task, he will make sure that it is completed. The university authorities held many meetings and still could not decide whether to expel or reprimand me. They finally decided that I would remain in university under observation but would no longer be registered as a student. When I finished my studies (without a diploma), I would be sent to the rural areas. I was overjoyed.

God granted me grace and opportunity. The most memorable part of my student life was the evangelism. I longed to spread the gospel even more than I longed to complete my studies. Very soon, the number of those who gathered around me seeking the truth increased. We divided into two groups, using holidays to hold fellowship in the park. We told others that we were conducting political studies. We continued in this way until graduation, unhindered by the authorities, who did not know of our activities. All the time our brothers and sisters were growing in their spiritual lives; by graduation, they were able to walk independently as mature Christians.

After graduation, we were sent from Altay to Kulum. We worked in virtually every major city in Xinjiang. I was sent to a farm to teach English, but I used my holidays to visit brothers and sisters scattered in different places. Although the road has not been as rough as the one my father walked 30 years ago, it has still been full of trials. Whenever I ride on a bus in the Xinjiang plateau, my heart is flooded with joy as I visualize the wheat field ready for harvest. When the seed is sowed in the ground, it gives birth to new life.

# Chapter 2

# Granny Jie

*In 1999, passing through southern Hebei province, Kim-kwong Chan came to a small church that held about four hundred people. He learned that more than one thousand people attended services every Sunday. He asked who was in charge, and the Christians took him to a small hut adjacent to the church building. The hut, a mere 12 square meters, had a large table in the center that served as the church office. Next to the table was a bed with an old lady sitting on it. Everyone called her Old Granny. Here is the story of the Zhaoxian (Zhao county) Church and ninety-five-year-old Granny Jie Lingmiao.*

Zhaoxian, formerly called Zhaozhou, is about twenty-five miles southeast of Shijiazhuang, the capital of Hebei. In the 1920s, two people from Zhaoxian went to a missionary hospital in Baoding City for medical treatment. Later they received Christ. Back in Zhaoxian, they started a clinic and a 'gospel hall' to spread the faith. In 1928, a Swedish missionary began working at that clinic. Soon there were about two hundred believers, and they started the Zhaoxian gospel hall. By 1949, there were between four and five hundred people coming every Sunday.

One of them was Granny Jie. One night in the early 1950s, as Jie Lingmiao prayed, she saw in a vision people moving pews and tables from the church onto a large truck. She went for a closer look. Then she heard a voice from the truck: 'Whom do you say that lady is? I'll tell you. She is Xiao Miao.' ('Little Miao' was Jie's name). Jie Lingmiao couldn't understand the meaning of this vision.

Soon, however, it became all too clear. God had revealed that persecution was coming soon. Christian gatherings were terminated and, as in her vision, everything in the church – chairs, hymnals, musical instruments – was confiscated. With the church closed, Christians suddenly became spiritual orphans, like sheep without a shepherd. They tearfully prayed, 'Lord, what sins have we committed? Why have you forsaken us?' Their cry seemed to be no more than a light whisper, and their Lord seemed so far away that he couldn't hear it.

In the church, those who were weak in faith gradually left. But not Granny Jie, whose faith only grew stronger: 'The will of God is like a mystery,' she said. 'Whatever things he desires are beyond our knowledge. Only one thing is certain: he will not forsake those who rely on him.'

She took upon herself the difficult task of pastor. Since it was not possible to hold meetings in the open, she conducted Christian services in secret. With large assemblies outlawed, she scattered Christians in many small groups to witness for the Lord. Villages and farms became her mission field. Through her, the gospel was spread all over Zhaoxian, and many were saved from their sins.

In the fall of 1961, as Granny Jie was walking to a village to share the gospel, she met a lady close to her own age who looked heartbroken. Granny Jie learned that this lady's daughter had been very ill for more than a year. The family had impoverished itself trying to find a cure, to no avail.

There seemed no way out. Granny Jie shared the gospel with the woman. They knelt in the field, praying for the mercy of Jesus Christ. Then Jie went with her new friend to visit the daughter, Zhao Yuge, who was as thin as straw. Jie shared the gospel with Miss Zhao's family, and they all prayed earnestly for her healing. Afterward, Jie visited her many times and prayed for her.

There was no improvement in Miss Zhao's condition, however. Granny Jie began to doubt her faith. In her struggle between faith and doubt, the Holy Spirit manifested his might. After a few days, the bedridden Miss Zhao began to get up and walk. Slowly her strength was restored, to the utter amazement of her neighbors. Miss Zhao became a faithful believer. During those years of calamities, God protected Granny Jie and she was a spiritual mentor to many people like Miss Zhao.

In 1962, the home of Zhao and her husband, Mr Fung, became the only Christian gathering point in the county. Meetings were held in secret. In 1963, Zhao gave birth to a boy, and God revealed that he should be named Moses. As Moses grew, the family prospered.

Meanwhile, Granny Jie was secretly leading several dozen more people to Christ. In 1970, the official government record conceded the existence of only 18 Christians in Zhaoxian.

One day in the early 1980s, the Christians read in the newspaper about a new government religious policy that allowed them to openly declare their faith and hold meetings. Granny Jie, now seventy-six, spread this good news around the county.

Yet many difficulties remained. In 1985, when the government finally agreed to return the church's property after over thirty years, the building was in ruins. The government's oversight was even more ruinous. The Religious

Affairs Bureau decided everything for the newly legal church. It appointed church leaders, authorized all church activities, and even approved the list of baptismal candidates.

The church became severely hindered. Worse, some officers, along with the government-appointed church leaders, privately sold off most of the church's property at a ridiculously low price so that the officers could build their own houses. Finally, the government only compensated the church with a small patch of land and a pittance for rebuilding.

The Christians were in tears as they prayed for the Lord's help. In December 1992, Granny Jie, along with many others, went to argue with the government officials. Their prayers were answered as they regained the right to elect their church leadership. Quickly the church expanded from several hundred to the current one thousand five hundred.

Even at ninety-five, Granny Jie can still hear, see and preach. She is seldom sick. Whenever she is ill, she always says, 'Lord Jesus will heal me.' Her confidence is rooted in experience. Many people have been healed following her prayers. Yet Jie has always said, 'I never pray for healing. I just preach the gospel of repentance in the name of our Lord. Only those who believe in Jesus can have their souls saved.'

Her daily prayer regimen starts at 5 a.m., as she prays for everyone who has made a request, even when she is ill. Every evening from 8 p.m. to 8.45 p.m., she kneels in prayer. While many of her young coworkers must move around after such a long stretch, Granny Jie is content. She has been kneeling in prayer for so many years that she has developed a thick callus on her knee. This mark signifies the kind of relationship she has with God.

Granny Jie also leads a daily women's prayer group at 4 p.m., to intercede for the ministry of the church and for her coworkers. Because of these prayers, the Zhaoxian Church prospers. Homes are restored and people are healed, yet Granny Jie has always said, 'Jesus says it is not my ability but his; it is really Jesus who has been saving people.'

After offering herself for ministry, Granny Jie has never taken a day off. She receives neither salary nor stipend from the church but trusts God for all her needs. She offered her life savings to build a new church, without leaving anything for herself or her relatives. Several years ago, Granny Jie decided that the Zhaoxian Church should have a building that could seat at least one thousand five hundred people. She also wanted a pastoral training center for lay leaders from rural churches in Zhaoxian and insisted that it should be built on the site of the local Communist Cadres Training Center. However, the poor Christians in this rural farming community had no money to finance her grand vision.

In 1999, the training institute went up for sale. It consisted of two long rows of two-storey buildings in a large courtyard. Fung Moses dreamed of putting a roof across these two buildings: the courtyard would become the sanctuary, while the buildings would be church offices and training center classrooms. Although this plan was totally beyond their financial ability, Granny Jie insisted that this would be the place.

Through what some might call a coincidence, some expatriate (mostly American) Christians living in Beijing recently heard about this project and have said they are willing to help pay for it. Perhaps the Communist Cadres Training Center will indeed be converted into a Christian Pastoral Training Center. This will be just the latest answered prayer for an old lady from Zhaoxian.

# Chapter 3

# Serenity in Calamity

*The Christian community in China has a strong witness of faith in difficult times. Christians, of course, suffer along with other Chinese in times of disaster. During political campaigns, Christians might suffer more than their neighbors. Yet with their faith in God, believers usually demonstrate a supernatural serenity before the larger society, one of their only ways to demonstrate the Christian faith publicly.*

*Pastor Yesu is the head of a vibrant community in Gongshan county at the Sino-Burmese border in northwest Yunnan. While he is a member of the Lisu people, Pastor Yesu ministers not only to the Lisus, but also to the Dulongs and the Nus. His account here describes the godly reactions of Christians to the loss by fire of their church building and homes. Church buildings are vital to Chinese Christians, being just about the only public means to proclaim their faith. Chinese believers must usually make great sacrifices to construct church buildings. The spirit of Nehemiah seems to be very lively among the Christians of China.*

*Chapter 4 describes Pastor Yesu's evangelistic activities among the Dulongs. Pastor Yesu has only a junior high school education and a few months of pastoral*

> *training on basic biblical knowledge. However, he*
> *is gifted in teaching, evangelism, and writing. Some*
> *of his articles have been published by the Chinese*
> *Christian journal* Tien Feng.
>      *For more on the Lisu Christians, see Appendix 2.*

In mid-November 1994, we were finishing the seventh annual pastoral training class at the Church of Yuege village, Pulade township. Some 126 students had come from more than forty churches and family meeting points from all over Gongshan county for three weeks of work and fellowship. Every day the students thirsted for the Word of God and participated in Bible studies, preaching, discussions and hymn singing; our joyful songs filled the whole village. It was a blessed, happy time. The Christians in this village took the students into their homes. They continually donated firewood, vegetables and rice to our training class so that we lacked nothing.

It was Saturday, the day before the graduation service, and everyone was busy getting ready. The kitchen was stocked with the next day's food. Exhausted, I managed to finish preparing my Sunday sermon as well as the order of service. Everyone came to the church for a service. Two of the sisters offered some hymns; the hymns were so moving that many joined the singing in tears.

Suddenly, someone yelled: 'Fire! Fire! Help us put out the fire!' Everyone made a rush for the tiny church door. Since I was at the pulpit, I was almost the last one out. As the coordinator of the training program, I was afraid that the fire might reach the dormitory, and my responsibility weighed on me heavily.

When I got out, I saw that the fire was at a non-Christian Lisu house in the village. This rather wealthy family had invited many friends to a drinking party. (Alcoholism is common among the Lisus, and most Lisu Christians abstain from drinking.) Those in the house were too drunk to fight the fire, but many of our students were already helping. Some tried to fetch water, while others attempted to retrieve the furniture. I ran over to help. Then I heard a man inside crying. He was drunk and could hardly walk. One of our students rushed in and carried him out. The man would have been burned alive had our student not rescued him.

In spite of our efforts, however, we could not extinguish the fire. The source of water was too far away, and we had to contend with a very strong wind. Soon, several other houses caught fire. We knew the battle was lost. Our students saved all the useful items they could from the burning homes, whether they belonged to Christians or not. We also saved a drunken old man from one of the houses where another family had also hosted a drinking party. This man, abandoned like the first, would have died if not for our students.

Quickly, the fire spread to more than 20 households. Two hours later, the local government organized a 200-person firefighting brigade, but it was too late. Soon all 36 homes in the village caught fire. With the strong wind, the whole village was in flames, and we were forced back. Complicating our efforts, some homes had dynamite and detonators, which sparked many explosions amid the inferno. It was the most furious fire that I have ever seen. It was like a big wave that swallowed the entire village.

That evening, many of us had to sleep on the road. Others went to the few houses at the bottom of the hill not affected by this fire. I stayed at another house where more than 40 of our students slept on the floor. I could not sleep at all. I wondered whether any of our students would accuse God of not taking care of us.

As the sun rose, I went back to the village. The daylight confirmed my worst fears. All the houses, and our church, were just ashes. All our food was gone. However, one of our deacons, whose house was spared at the edge of the village, immediately donated more than one hundred pounds of rice, which was all the food he had, to our students. We gratefully and hungrily ate the rice after the whole evening of firefighting.

All the non-Christians were crying aloud, beating their chests, but all the Christians came as usual for the Sunday service. We sat on the ashes, sang hymns, prayed, and encouraged each other. However, I could not say anything and simply wept instead. Yet I was comforted knowing that we were quietly holding our Sunday worship service to praise God, in spite of all that had happened.

At noon, the students returned to their villages. The deacons gathered all the Christians of Yuege for an afternoon service at one of the few houses that had been spared. They invited me to preach, but I had nothing to say. Instead, the elder spoke on my behalf, using the Bible to comfort and encourage.

On Monday, many Christians from other villages came carrying food, clothing and money to share with their brothers and sisters who had lost everything. I gathered my church coworkers to discuss how to distribute the donations. All the deacons said, 'The most urgent thing that we need now is the church; let us pour all these donations into rebuilding our church.' In the evening, we gathered all the Christians in Yuege to share this decision; every Christian supported this idea, saying, 'We can make do, temporarily, without our homes. But we must have a place to gather for worship.'

Quickly we purchased the materials. As Christians heard about the needs of the church, they stopped their own home rebuilding and joined us in rebuilding the church. They chose to live in tents so that the rebuilding project could finish sooner. More than one hundred people worked at the building site every day. They carried stones, sand and cement. Some donated yams to feed the volunteers. Soon the church was finished.

From the day the church was burned down until the day it was rebuilt, no other Christians shed a tear. They proceeded as if the destruction were just an ordinary event. However, when we held the dedication service for our new building, many of them wept. These were not tears of sadness but of thankfulness and joy. Through calamities and trials, the Lord opened our eyes and affirmed our faith so that we could see his grace. The fire left the Christians of Yuege with nothing but their lives, but they saw the love of God and the love of other Christians in action. Before the fire, the church was of very simple construction, with planks and sticks. After the fire, it was a much more solid church, literally and figuratively.

After the fire, many non-Christians blamed heaven for not caring for them; some lamented their losses loudly. But none of the Christians who were afflicted blamed God. Rather, they remained serene, as if these were ordinary days. They continued gathering to sing hymns and pray. They still had fun in their daily lives. It is no surprise, then, that the non-Christians around them saw their peace and joy. Many were baptized and joined our church. Today, there are more Christians in Yuege than ever. The Bible truly says, 'And we know that in all things God works for the good of those who love him' (Rom. 8:28).

# Chapter 4

# Beautiful Feet

*The Dulongs are one of the smallest minority groups in China, with perhaps five thousand people. Most of them (almost four thousand) live in the Dulong valley – a place that was not accessible by road until the year 2000. Theirs is perhaps the last frontier in China. Before the road, the only way to get to them was by climbing for three days through a narrow trail. This path is usually closed by snow from mid-October until the following May. So for six months every year the Dulongs were cut off from the rest of the world.*

*Dulong village is one of the poorest townships in Yunnan province. Its people, who are farmers, are barely able to survive. The government must subsidize all of the township's social services and every year must send in, by horse or by donkey, hundreds of tons of daily supplies such as oil, salt, batteries and so on, so that the Dulongs can get through the winter.*

*In the 1940s, a Lisu evangelist named Bolaw went into the southern part of the Dulong valley to preach the gospel, and he established a church there. Later, an American missionary, Joseph Morse, also served there briefly. By 1950, a small Christian community had been established in the southern Dulong valley* with its own pastor, Elijah. However, he had moved out of the valley in the late 1980s. Nothing more was known of the Dulong Christians until 1991, when six of them went to Gongshan, to a pastoral training institute. This proved that the Dulong Christians had kept their faith for more than forty years without any outside help. Several hundred strong, they had established several gathering points for Christian worship.

The Dulong valley is naturally divided into southern and northern parts. All Dulong Christians live at the southern part of the valley. Although the gospel had been introduced into the valley more than fifty years before, not a single Christian had been to the northern part to share the gospel.

As the Lisu Christians heard the encouraging news about the Dulong Christians, they were overjoyed. The Dulongs pleaded with their Lisu brethren to run a pastoral training program for them. In 1995 and 1996, the Church in Gongshan sent pastors to the valley to conduct training sessions. In November 1996, Pastor Yesu went there to survey the Christian population. Elder John of the Dulong Church then asked Pastor Yesu to bring an evangelistic team to the northern part of the valley.

This was a huge challenge for the Christians of Gongshan. They have little, other than their simple faith. The church leaders decided to do pioneer mission work in 1997. The evangelists would have to carry all their supplies from Gongshan on their backs. Their food, medicine, salt, blankets, oil, torches and Bibles would have to last for the entire journey. It would not be a task for the weak, physically or spiritually.

Below, Pastor Yesu tells of this first mission trip to the northern Dulong valley, the 'last frontier' in China.

*He wrote it in December 1997, shortly after the journey, in Kunming, Yunnan. For more on the Lisu Christians, see Chapter 3 and Appendix 2.*

On 12 September 1997, two Dulong brothers came to my home to escort us to the Dulong valley for a pastoral training class. After a couple of days' rest (they had been walking for three days already), we left on the 15th. However, heavy rains washed out the road and made us turn back. We finally started off again on the 17th, knowing that our hosts were anxiously waiting for us. In the evening, we reached the first main post on the road – Jidu. This is just a piece of flat ground with a small spring nearby. We pitched our tent. One of us went for firewood; another washed the rice to cook the meal. Later, the sky turned dark, and there was a terrific thunderstorm.

We got up at 4 a.m. the next morning, and it was still raining. Unable to cook, we ate a few biscuits and started hiking at 5 a.m., using flashlights because it was still dark. After a stop for breakfast three hours later, we continued our journey until we arrived in Mingliwa, where we pitched our tents for the night.

On the third day, we reached the Dulong valley and came to the Mabede Church, the main church. Sixty students were waiting for us. The houses in Mabede village are scattered widely. Our training program consisted of courses in basic doctrine and pastoral work. We also held a Dulong literacy class every day. The government supported our program because of its policy to have all national minority groups literate in their own languages.

The training class ended on 6 October. We then got ready to travel to the northern part of the valley, to do evangelism. We had gathered medicine, oil and more than two hundred pounds of rice. Our team was composed of three porters, a local guide, two cooks, a Dulong language instructor and folklorist, and four evangelists. The porters took us as far as Dulongwu village.

After we crossed Shilalu into the northern part of the valley, we entered a jungle with very few inhabitants. We walked for half a day and could only spot a few households. I felt a bit scared, as we were alone. My mood was not improved when we had to cross a rapid current on a wire bridge consisting of a few broken wooden planks. We just barely made it to the other side of the river safely.

In the evening, we arrived at Kungmu village, a composite of three smaller villages. As we entered, we noticed that the houses were very different from the Dulong houses in the southern part of the valley. They were shorter, smaller, dirtier, and rather poorly kept. We tried to find a place to stay, but most of the families were crowded into one small room for each home. At last we found an empty house, but it was only one and a half meters high. We had to stoop before we could enter, and we always had to be careful not to hit our heads on the ceiling (which we did anyway). The room was filthy, so we spent some time cleaning it out. The owner gave us some firewood we could burn to mask the terrible smell.

After supper, we invited people to our evangelistic meeting. About twenty showed up to hear my sermon. We began with Elder John, the Dulong language instructor. Although Elder John was over sixty, he was still very healthy. Before the cultural revolution he had been a preacher, but after 1950 he worked at the Ministry of Culture. When Elder John was young, he learned the Lisu language; later, he learned Chinese. Through many years of effort, Elder John had created the Dulong scripts. He was a genius. He was also a great storyteller. That evening, he recounted the traditional Dulong epics. Dulongs love to hear their folklore and are proud of their epics. One cannot be considered a real Dulong if he or she cannot recall the Dulong epics.

The retelling of these epics can last for several days. Since I could not understand the language, I did not know what Elder John had told the audience. But I knew that all were captivated by his stories. Some asked questions, and he spoke for two hours. Finally, he told them that it was time to hear a new story – the good news of the Christian religion. I asked my interpreter what I should speak about. He replied, 'What John said tonight had lots of similarities with the story of creation in Genesis. You should begin with Genesis.' So I spoke of God's creation of mankind, his commissioning mankind to rule over creation, and the Fall, with the resulting eternal damnation of mankind. Further, I also talked about God's plan of salvation, faith, and the benefits of accepting the gospel. I also talked about the government's religious policy.

Then I noticed that my interpreter was tired, so I stopped preaching. But as soon as I did, the people asked me to teach them some hymns, because they had never heard any. Then I sang several hymns for them. Finally, I stood up and asked, 'Would anyone like to accept Jesus tonight? If so, please stand up, and I'll pray for you.' Nobody stood up. A few women said, 'We can't decide tonight. We have to think about it. We hope that you can come back and tell us more about your religion so that we can accept Jesus.'

That night, some of our coworkers were disheartened. However, I believed that the seed had been sown and that one day it would germinate and bear fruit. Then we would be overjoyed.

At sunrise the next day, we started our journey, leaving some rice and oil for our return. We walked for ten hours. At night, we reached Dalesu village. Mr Lung Guangzhong gave us his house while he moved to the barn. Immediately, we started cleaning up the place, cooking supper, and going door to door to invite people to our meeting. That evening, my interpreter was not feeling very well, so I only spoke for an hour and a half. But when I asked who would like to accept Jesus, nine people stood up. I prayed for them and committed them into the hands of God. Because there was no pastor, only God could minister their needs and lead them into maturity. My coworkers taught them to sing some hymns. After a long time, they could sing the short Lisu hymn 'Come to Jesus'.

On the morning of 9 October, we departed, again leaving some rice and oil for our return. As we headed further north, the road became more difficult. The whole area was a jungle, and no sunlight reached us. At noon, we arrived at Dalungwu village. There, two of the porters returned to their home. Elder John and a Christian brother would stay at this village for a while to promote Dulong literacy. The rest of us continued north.

Late at night, we arrived at Dadezhengdan village. It was rather large, but the houses were minuscule. The administrative office was locked, so we tried the village store and were glad to discover that the owner was from the same southern village as one of our coworkers, James De. In fact, the store owner's wife was also from the south. She had been one of my students when I held my first pastoral training class in Dulong valley in 1994. Later, married in this remote place and without any Christian fellowship, her faith had begun to cool. However, she and the store owner received us with warm hospitality.

We held an evangelistic meeting there and slept there. Not many people came to our meeting because they were very afraid of us, the outsiders. Only six showed up, and one, the local doctor, accepted Christ. He could read

Chinese, so we gave him a Chinese Bible, a hymnal, and a Christian magazine.

The next day it was raining. We covered ourselves with plastic sheets and continued our journey. At night, we reached Dahongdan village and stayed at the house of the chief. This man had two rooms, but also ten family members, so in all we had 17 people there. It was still raining, but our coworkers went door to door inviting people to come. About twenty did, but because the room was so small, we had to put our luggage and furniture outside to make room for the audience. It was worth the inconvenience. That night, none of the people refused Jesus, and the chief even promised that he would lead the village (more than one hundred people) to accept Jesus. At bedtime, he gave us his bed, while he and his family slept on the floor, covered by a plastic sheet.

The following morning, 11 October, we planned to head to the northernmost village. However, the rain got heavier, and it had even begun snowing at the top of the mountain. If the road was impassable, we would not be able to return. We were also running out of food because we had shared so much of it with the poor Dulong people wherever we went. Our cook calculated that our provisions would last for just four more days. Moreover, our medic told us that we had run out of medicine. Therefore, we concluded that we must head back south along the river.

As our decision to leave reached the villagers, more than fifty showed up, asking to hear more about the gospel. I preached a simple message, prayed for them, and committed them into the hands of God. They stood along the road to say farewell. As we reached the other side of the mountain, we could see that they were still standing in the rain, watching us. Oh, they were like a flock of sheep without a shepherd! This place was remote, and there was no one to minister to them. It took a round trip of 20 days just to walk to the county seat from here. However, I trusted that God had heard our prayer. We had sowed the seed of the gospel among them. God would personally lead them and care for their needs. We continue to hope that God will raise up some spiritual leaders among these new Christians.

Trying to compress two days of walking into one, we jogged all the way to Dalesu. We arrived at 10 p.m. and stayed at Mr Lung's home. Many people were waiting for our preaching. Elder John, who had stayed at Dalungwu village, had led two more to Christ, bringing the total to 11. Two coworkers took turns teaching them hymns until 1 a.m. Exhausted because of our daylong run, we had to convince them to go home. On Sunday morning we worshiped God together.

In the afternoon, we left for Dilan village, which was rather large. There was a small school building next to it. The teacher was from Maku, in the south. This teacher, Ms Jiang Guoying, had picked up some basic knowledge of Christianity in Maku. She invited us to her home for tea and even brought us a chicken, which we cooked in her kitchen. Ms Jiang let us use the classroom for our evening meeting, since there were no other rooms large enough in the whole village. Afterwards, I told the people to think about their decision overnight and tell us in the morning whether they would like to accept Jesus.

As we were lying down, many people with torches came to our place, pleading with us to preach more. One of them, bringing us a chicken and some yam, said, 'I have lived in this place my whole life, and never have I heard such good news. In spite of many difficulties, you came from far away to share this good news with us. I really thank you from the bottom of my heart. This is a token of our gratitude.'

We got up and took turns preaching and teaching them hymns.

In the morning, nine people came to our place wanting to accept Jesus and asking us to pray for them. As we were about to leave, Ms Jiang brought all her students and asked us to take a picture with my camera. As I looked at those students lining up for the picture, I began to cry. None had a pair of shoes; their clothes were rags and didn't even cover them. I took a closer look at the school. It had a classroom, the kitchen and Ms Jiang's bedroom. The walls were wooden planks, while the roof was just hay. It looked like a rundown shed that might collapse with a heavy snow. It was so small and so poorly equipped that many of the students had to stand all day in class. I admired Ms Jiang, who was just twenty-five. Her salary was hardly enough to feed her. Yet she loved her students and had committed herself to this place.

On 13 October, we left, reaching Xianjiudan village in the evening. We stayed at the chief's home and held an evangelistic meeting for about thirty people. The chief was the first to stand up and receive Jesus. Later, 17 more made the decision. Some could read Chinese, so we left a few Bibles and hymnals behind.

The following morning we left for Baikawa village. There were about a dozen houses, but we could not find a suitable place to stay for the night. We had walked all day without food, and we were exhausted. I just sat on the ground. Finally, a couple took us into their small hut. After dinner, we held the meeting. Only 20 came, because many had gone out hunting. However, 10 decided to accept Jesus.

On the morning of 15 October, our cook told us that we only had enough food for breakfast. We had to reach Mabede village that day, so we ran all the way back. By nighttime we reached Elder John's home. The Christians had been waiting for us. We told them about our evangelistic expedition and prayed for all those who had accepted Christ. We rested there for a day and were finally ready to leave Dulong valley. However, Pastor Di of the Lawadu Church invited us to join in a thanksgiving service. So we spent a whole day at Lawadu, full of joy and thankfulness.

We left Dulong valley on 20 October, reaching home on the 22nd. We had been on the road for 37 days. By mid-November, the snow came, and the only road to Dulong valley was closed off. The Dulongs would remain in their isolated world for another six months. Yet now in that valley are many brothers and sisters in Christ, whom I love. May the Lord protect them, and may they enjoy peace and joy.

# Chapter 5

# Opium and the Gospel

*Opium and the gospel have always had a peculiar relationship in China.*

*China was forced to open to foreign trade through the Opium War in the mid-nineteenth century. Missionaries tagged along with merchants and enjoyed special privileges. Some of the earliest Protestant missionaries also served with the East India Company – the primary opium trader.*

*Ironically, one of the biggest social contributions by missionaries in China in the late nineteenth century was the rehabilitation of opium addicts through the gospel. Even more ironic, in 1950 the Communist government declared that religion, including Christianity, is the opiate of the people.*

*By the mid-1950s, the government had successfully eradicated opium addiction in China through rehabilitation programs. China began adopting a variety of economic reforms, starting in the early 1980s. While the economic situation greatly improved, all kinds of social problems – such as prostitution and gambling – began to surface. Currently, one of the most serious social pathologies in China is drug abuse, as opium addiction has returned with a vengeance. It is par-*

*ticularly significant in the parts of Yunnan where opium
is grown and is cheap. In some villages, not only are
all of the villagers opium farmers, they are opium
addicts.*

*The government has tried many things to combat
the problem, with limited success. One of its most
successful methods has been through a partnership with
the Christian faith, the 'opiate of the people'. Some
officials have concluded that Christianity can help build
a civilized society through its sound moral teachings.
Hostility toward Christianity has decreased, as the
Communists, at least in some cases, have used the moral
strength of Christianity to combat crime.*

*This chapter provides translations of official letters
showing how the government has actually helped
promote Christianity to combat opium addiction in
southwestern Yunnan province.*

Lancan Lahu autonomous county, at the western tip of
Simao prefecture, is next to the infamous 'Golden Triangle'
area of Burma (Myanmar), Thailand, and China. Although
it is illegal in China to plant opium, there has been no
effective law enforcement in remote areas, such as Lancan
county. The prefecture government tried to eradicate the
problem but failed, partly because most of the farmers
made more money planting opium than traditional crops.
However, as more opium was planted, more opium addicts
were harvested. A negative economic cycle quickly kicked
in, more than canceling out the wealth generated by opium
planting. Making matters worse, the traditional religious
practice of sacrificing livestock to treat illnesses forced many
families into poverty when their members got ill as addicts.

The local government began noticing that those who
became Christians usually were wealthier than their neigh-

bors because they did not participate in the traditional costly livestock sacrifice. Moreover, virtually none were involved with drugs. Also, Christians neither drank nor smoke.

The government decided on a two-pronged approach: to promote Christianity, in order to gradually replace the folk religion and its costly practices, and to introduce Christianity among opium addicts. A small village – Gaozhiba – was chosen as the site of the pilot project. The findings of this experiment have been published in an academic journal in China (The Nanjing University Institute of Religious Studies, *Religion* [1998], issues 3 and 4), where they were interpreted as a positive use of religion for the construction of socialist China.

The Lahus in that region have traditionally been polytheists and animists. Their unique folk religion has been mistakenly labeled Buddhism. Lahu priests, called *mubus*, are brought in to offer sacrificial animals to various deities during transitional points in life. Additionally, Lahus see all kinds of natural abnormalities as the result of evil, also requiring sacrifice. If someone gets sick, Lahus must kill chickens until the signs become positive. This costs lots of money. In 1991, Gaozhiba sacrificed 10 oxen, 20 pigs and more than 100 chickens to the deities – an astronomical amount of wealth in a village of several hundred people. These practices, not surprisingly, are one of the causes of poverty in the region.

Christianity was introduced to this village in early 1992. Soon these Christians were doing better financially than the non-Christians around them. Why? The Christians did not need to sacrifice any animals. Then the government encouraged the *mubus* to study Christianity. Gradually, some of them became Christian preachers among the Lahus. The Christians began to implement new farming techniques advocated by the government and did still better. As of

1998, there were 58 Christian families (with 69 baptized Christians and more than 200 people undergoing Christian instruction). Most of these families built new roofs and purchased new waterproof huts. They also built a church that could hold 300 people. Christianity has become the predominant religion in the village and is now regarded as a driving force for economic prosperity.

A second area of concern was drug-related crime. In the past, Gaozhiba was famous for three 'lots': lots of drug addicts, lots of thieves, and lots of lazy people. The local government not only educated residents about the law, it began promoting Christian moral teachings, such as the Ten Commandments, that do not contradict with socialist tenets. Many of the drug addicts have since given up their addictions upon conversion. Local gangsters Li Cun and Zheng Ci were notorious drug abusers, bullies, and thieves. Everyone hated and feared them. After they became Christians, however, the church began supervising their conduct. They now live normal lives.

Following this successful experiment, the county employed the same strategy in other drug-infected villages. Of course, it could not publicize these efforts. It would be embarrassing if people knew that Christianity could achieve something that socialism couldn't. Although the local government's program was not publicized beyond the few villages involved, the following two letters tell about it. Readers can draw their own conclusions.

## 1 Baishidi village

To the Religious and National Minority Affairs Bureaus of the county government and of the prefecture government:

Our village has 54 households and 234 people. Historically, we have believed in Buddhism. In the name of Buddhist religion, we have slaughtered pigs and cows to send the evil spirits away. Many families have had all their pigs and oxen killed and live in poverty. We also have many opium addicts among us.

From 15 November to 30 December 1997, we gathered all the opium addicts, forcing them to give up their drug habit. We promoted the government's 'Decisions and Regulations to Stop Opium' document and also the policy on freedom of religious belief in our national constitution. We organized the cultural propaganda team of the village government and invited the propaganda [evangelistic] teams from the Laba and Habo Christian churches to speak to these addicts.

At the same time, we actively promoted the good testimonies of the Christian families from the churches of Laba and Habo. We told them that the lives of these Christians have been changed by this religion, and they now could afford to have waterproof asbestos roofs, with some even able to purchase television sets, tape recorders and sewing machines.

Through these practical illustrations, many Buddhist believers wanted to convert to Christian faith. Between 1998 and November 1999, we have had 29 families, a total of 91 persons, become Christians. Sixty-six of them were baptized. [Pedobaptism is not allowed in China.] During the past two years, all of these new Christians experienced lifestyle improvements. For example, Mr Li Muguo and his family slaughtered two pigs and two oxen to send the evil spirits away and had no animals left. Two years after they converted to Christian faith, they have three oxen and four pigs. They have already sold two pigs to gain RMB 300 yuan and 15 chickens to earn another RMB 300 yuan.

On 15 April 1998, we built a 60-square-meter tent, with an oilcloth roof, for Christian gatherings. The tent is already leaking, and we need to build one with an asbestos roof. But our economic situation is still not very ideal. We can chip in with our labors and with lumber, but we can't come up with RMB 2,500 [$400] to purchase 80 asbestos roof sheets and nails. We hope that the relevant government ministries can help us with the money. We make our application in this letter.

Baishidi Church Administrative Committee
Village Administrative Office
Village Religious Affairs Committee, 28 December 1999

*[Official seal of the village government, with the following signed comment: 'The situation is acute; please help.']*

*[Official seal of the district government, with the following signed comment: 'The situation is acute. We hope that the relevant government departments can give us help.']*

*[Official seal of the Religious and National Minority Affairs Bureau of the county government, with the signed comment: 'The situation is acute. However, we have no resources to help. We ask the prefecture government to extend the assistance, 29 December 1999.']*

## 2  Banguode village

County and prefecture government officers:

Our village has about one hundred and ten families with more than four hundred and thirty people. Historically, we have believed in the Buddhist religion. Whenever someone is sick, we invite the *mubu* to perform liturgies, and we must offer oxen and pigs to send away the evil spirits. Fifty years after the Liberation, most of us still live in poverty. Many of us smoke opium and trade opium. In December 1997, we had 64 opium addicts in our village. Our village has had perhaps one of the largest number of drug addicts among the villages of this area.

We must eradicate the drug problem, as ordered by the National People's Congress, and affirm the policy of freedom of religious belief. We gathered all our drug addicts at the village administrative office from 15 November to 30 December 1997, forcing them to give up this habit. During this detention period, we invited the propaganda team from the Laba and Habo Christian churches to work among those addicts. At the same time, we promoted the policy of freedom of religious belief and demanded that the religious believers be well versed in their faith.

Religious believers show improvements in their lives. We share the many testimonies of those Christians from Laba and Habo of the improvements they have experienced since they accepted the Christian religion. From these efforts, 56 of the addicts stopped smoking opium. Five have become Christians.

From January 1998 until November 1999, we have had 43 households with 165 people accept Christianity, and there are 70 baptized believers. Many of them have since started raising pigs and oxen. Some even built new asbestos roofs. One of the ex-addicts, Li Sanmei, sold an ox and a pig for RMB 1,200. He donated RMB 800 to the church to purchase a new generator.

In April 1998, we built an 80-square-meter temporary hut as a church. It is leaking now, and we need to build a 120-square-meter church. We have pooled our resources and still lack RMB 3,000 to purchase asbestos roof tiles. We hope that you can help us.

*[Seal and comments are similar to those in the previous letter.]*

These two letters, along with two similar applications, were sent to the Simao prefecture Religious and National Minority Affairs Bureau, which transferred this request to the Yunnan Christian Council. Private donations designated for these projects were sent from Hong Kong to the Simao prefecture government via the Yunnan Christian Council. The construction projects were completed by June 2000.

These cases suggest that Christianity is a significant social force that the Chinese authorities can no longer ignore. Indeed, they even try to co-opt this moral force for the benefit of society. Clearly, the government can no longer interpret Christianity according to the classic Marxist view, as the opiate of the people. Instead, Christianity has become, at least in some areas, a means to combat opium. This development may force socialist theoreticians to reexamine the ideological basis of religion. This, in turn, could challenge the core belief system of the Chinese government.

It all began with a few simple believers who broke the bondage of opium addiction with the transforming power of the gospel. These simple, yet profound experiences have transformed many hitherto non-Christian communities into Christian villages.

# Chapter 6

# A Lifelong Servant of God

*Some of God's servants have been called to spread the gospel in China's remote regions. Many new Christian communities have been born out of their hunger, torture, illness, jail, loneliness, poverty and humiliation. They embody the spiritual strength of the church in China – endurance in suffering. Lu Bingzhi, now in her nineties, was like thousands of Chinese evangelists who overcame the fiery trials of the twentieth century to lead many to Christ through their words and lives. Below are some of the fragments of events critical in Lu's spiritual journey, as told to Rev Yang Meiyong of Kunming, Yunnan.*

In 1909, Lu Bingzhi was born to Christian parents in Shangdong province, eastern China. Despite their prayers, Lu refused to accept Christianity. Once when she heard her father praying for her salvation, this high school girl angrily said, 'I will not believe this Jesus, which you believe in.'

Very soon, however, an ulcer developed on her left leg. It began to grow, and her family could not pay for medical treatment. Soon, the doctors recommended amputation to save her life. Her parents earnestly asked God to spare their daughter from becoming a handicapped person. Strong-willed but desperate, Lu also knelt with her parents to pray for God's mercy and to confess her sins. Her leg was completely healed, and Lu realized that she had to accept this Jesus. Lu knew that her previous anti-Christian words were spoken in ignorance, but she would not dare to offend her Creator again, and she committed her life, suddenly transformed, to this God of mercy. She became a messenger of the Good News she had received.

At this time, China was racked by civil war between various warlords and between the Communists and the Nationalists. Eventually, Lu traveled to northwestern China. For a while, she conducted evangelistic ministries at seven university campuses, leading students to Christ. However, the Nationalists suspected her of being a Communist agent, organizing underground cells among the students. Without any investigation, they arrested Lu and sentenced her to death.

The jailer told her, 'I sympathize for you, for you are so young. We have to execute you very soon. I can pass on a message to your parents if you wish.' Lu replied, 'I am innocent. I preach Jesus Christ, not politics. If my God is not willing (for me to die), not one single hair of mine will fall on the ground. I will not die.'

Fu Zuoyi, the northwestern regional commissioner general, heard of the death sentence given to a young lady and asked to see her. After he interviewed Lu, General Fu said, 'This is a preacher of Christian religion. We should not execute her and should immediately release her.' Lu's confident trust in her God had been well placed. The governor, apologetic, even hosted a dinner in her honor.

God protected Lu in various ways. Once, during winter, she was on her way to do evangelism. For some reason, the horse she was riding would not go on the road but only on a frozen river bed. Lu tried to pull the horse back to the road, but it would not yield. Later, however, it returned to the road. Lu could not understand why. Just after that, some Christians at the roadside welcomed Lu, telling her that a group of bandits had been waiting by the way. In fact, some travelers had just been robbed. Lu was convinced that God had sidetracked the horse to spare her.

When Lu was twenty-two, she rode alone on a white horse to Saerqin in Inner Mongolia to preach the gospel. 'Many people tried to convince me not to go there alone because there were many bandits there, and they would do all kinds of evil things,' she said. 'It would be very dangerous. But, after prayer, I started my journey.'

In the area were some notorious bandits from Shangdong, led by a man called Big Pox Liu. The government had tried to suppress them without success. As Lu rode on, she came upon a group of men. 'They ordered me to dismount from the horse and saw that I was a girl,' she recalled. 'They said, "What are you doing?" I replied, "I am an evangelist preaching the gospel of Jesus Christ." They said: "How can a young girl like you preach?" I boldly said, "Step aside and let me pass, otherwise the bandits will come." They laughed and said, "We are the bandits! You just bumped into us today." Then I pleaded, "Let me go. If you do not believe me, come to Saerqin Town tomorrow and hear my preaching." I also told them that I was from Shangdong. They said that since this young girl was from Shangdong, they would come to hear what kind of teaching I would offer.'

The bandits let her go. The following day, they came to Lu's preaching station. Then the whole gang, led by Big Pox Liu, knelt down and cried, confessing all their sins. Next they asked Lu: 'What shall we do now?' She told them to surrender their weapons to the government, so they went to see Inner Mongolia's provincial governor. They told him that after hearing this Shangdong girl's message of Jesus, they wanted to surrender and start a new life. Surprised, the governor declared that the government would accept their surrender. He pardoned them and gave them a piece of land to farm.

The change in Liu and his people was real. They had a good harvest after the first year and offered it to the government as an expression of their sincerity. The governor, however, declined to accept the harvest, knowing that they would need it. He even exempted them from land tax for the first three years. Liu and his people worked hard to show their repentance. They also led 300 people to Christ. There was peace in that region, and God's name was glorified.

In 1942, Lu attended the Jinan Bible School; later, she transferred to North China Theological Seminary. When time permitted, Lu and her classmates would do evangelistic work in the countryside. In 1946, she was a faculty member at the Nanjing Huangnegang Theological Seminary. She was also in charge of the devotional ministry in 11 schools in Nanjing. The work was busy and tiring, but her preaching was powerful, and many came to Christ.

One day, while praying, she saw a map of China in a vision. Soon, everything on it faded except Kunming City in Yunnan. Lu knew that the Lord was leading her there and shared her vision with her coworkers. Some joined her.

In 1948, Lu and her coworkers arrived at Kunming. Soon, they rented a place on Wuguo Road and started preaching. Many people accepted the Lord, and soon Lu and company had to find a larger place. The believers kept increasing in number. In 1952, two years after the Communist Party came to power, Lu and her coworkers bought a long hall with 13 houses so that more people would hear the gospel. Soon after, however, the meetings were banned, and Lu and many other pastors were arrested.

Imprisoned, Lu became ill. As her health improved, she was transferred to a prison farm. Despite heart and stomach problems, every day she had to collect a certain amount of tea leaves from the mountain. Work began at 6 a.m. and ended at 8 p.m. If she could not fulfill her quota, she would be punished. One winter evening, Lu finished rather late. Alone, she met five wolves on the road. At that moment, all she could do was pray, asking the Lord for strength. He told her: 'Do not be afraid, for I am with you. They will not harm you.' As Lu watched, the wolves simply stared at her as she walked past. One by one, they left.

Another day, Lu went to pick tea leaves on a cliff over a deep, rocky valley. There wasn't anyone around. She slipped, but some branches protruding from the cliff stopped her fall and spared her life, knocking out eight of her teeth in the process. Her face bloodied from the impact, Lu fainted. After she awoke, she climbed back on the cliff and began limping to the camp, using a stick as a crutch. Her face was badly scraped, and she had broken her arm. Because it was so late, everyone back in camp thought that Lu must have been killed. However, at midnight, Lu showed up, and the people admitted that her God had once again saved her life. Slowly her wounds healed.

In 1979, after more than twenty years of hard labor at the prison farm, Lu wrote this poem:

> As I look back on the path behind me,
> It was full of ups and downs.
> When I look forth into the future,
> It will still be rough and bumpy.
> However, only if I walk with the strength from God,
> The roads ahead will be full of glory.

Seventy years of living is like a dream.
What is left is a useless body, all beaten-up.
It is so heartbreaking.
As I feel the pain in my heart, I am awake again.
I only see the righteous seeds of the gospel.
They are now bearing fruits and flowers.
I'll uplift my heart.
I'll press forward with my fragile feet.
I will not stop till I reach Paradise.
I will not pause even when I pass a resting place.
I just know that I have to fight to the end.
Until one day when I cannot even drag myself up,
I know this is when one of my feet will have already
    stepped into Paradise.
The angels will surely lift me up.
As I open my eyes, I will see the merciful face of my
    Lord.
My heart will fill with contentment beyond words.
Nothing can separate me from Him.
There will be gold harps to accompany the choir.
Everlasting alleluia forever!

Lu was released from jail in 1979 as the government relaxed its control over religion. However, there was no place for Lu to go to. She had no family, no money, and no home. A nurse, Sister Yong, decided to take Madam Lu into her home, despite her own heavy family burdens. This was a beautiful testimony to all the neighbors. Sister Yong was later ordained and now serves the Holy Trinity Church in Kunming. Madam Lu, for her part, conducts a Bible study every day, teaching and exhorting whoever comes to her place, which is a gathering point for Christian worship in a church-operated retirement hostel.

# Chapter 7

# Signs and Wonders

*In Chinese folk religion, illness is caused by evil spirits or the gods to punish those who commit immoral deeds. Often the afflicted seek spiritual remedies, such as sacrifices, to break the bondage of evil powers or calm the wrath of the divine. Thus, pragmatism is a basic element of Chinese culture, especially in rural society.*

*When Christianity is introduced in the countryside, people measure its validity both on its ability to deliver miracles – especially to heal the sick – and on the magnitude of the punishments meted out by its God on believers who violate his commandments. If the God of the Christian faith performs miracles that confer benefits on his followers, people are inclined to replace their original deities with this new God. Of course, once they have switched allegiances, they expect God to reward them for doing good things and punish them when they deviate from Christian teaching.*

*This kind of Old Testament approach underlies the religiosity in many rural Chinese Christian communities. Signs and miracles are commonly found among them. Most of their members can provide testimonies of healing and other miracles. Very often, people turn to Christianity because they experience a physical deliverance from illness or affliction, and their faith gravitates to these testimonies.*

*The following stories all come from a small town in southern Fujian province. Christianity was introduced to this region almost a hundred years ago, but only in the larger cities and towns. The small towns and villages have been basically unreached.*

*During the late 1980s, there was a Christian woman, Wu Shining, who earned good money as a bus station manager for the county. She had accepted the Christian faith because her mother was a Christian, but she did not go to church much, choosing instead to invest her time in the pursuit of wealth. One day, however, she was so sick she could not get out of bed. Despite consultations with many doctors, there was no improvement. One night she decided God was punishing her because she worshiped money, so she asked him for forgiveness.*

*The next day, she got out of bed, completely healed. This woman dedicated herself to serving God, not money. She had saved enough money to go to seminary for a year. In 1990, she returned to the county and began evangelizing in the countryside. Many have received Christ through her ministry. In 1996 alone, she and her coworkers led more than sixty families to turn from their traditional folk religious practices to faith in Christ. Below, she describes just a few of the conversions that occurred in 1996. Pastor Wu, like many Chinese preachers, likes to lace her stories with quotations from Scripture.*

The four members of the Wei family lived in Tade village, where nobody had any contact with Christianity. Like many who live in the dark, the Weis were in turmoil from Satan's evil power. The son, Mulin, who was twenty-five, had suffered from a severe stomach problem for years. He could not eat anything. Whenever he did, he would vomit up the food. Doctors had tried different treatments, but there was no improvement. Then he had blood in his stools. He went to hospitals for treatment but, again, experienced no improvement. As the Bible says, 'Whoever believes in the Son has eternal life, but whoever rejects the Son will not see life, for God's wrath remains on him' (Jn. 3:36). Mulin had suffered for almost seven years, and his family had spent a lot of money. His mother was so worried that she became ill and needed bed rest.

The father, Pushi, aged sixty-three, had to slave in the fields to earn money for all the medical bills. Yet, despite his efforts, he was in debt. One day, while tending his ox, the animal suddenly knocked him down and stepped on him, breaking three of his ribs. Old Wei was sent to the hospital for emergency treatment. After he was discharged, he suffered a leg problem and could not walk.

God's love, however, was about to come upon this family. On 22 February, the mother, Lin Suiyu, aged sixty, and her son went to the county hospital because Mulin was so thin that he looked like a skeleton. The doctor told her, 'There is no treatment for Mulin.' As mother and son left with heavy hearts, they passed by the home of Dr Tu Yili's family, which had been Christian for several generations. The Spirit of the Lord moved the wife of Dr Tu, Sister Lanzai, to share the precious gospel with them. She also brought them to my home to listen to the gospel again. That night, I took them to one of our services, and our coworkers laid hands on them, praying for their healing.

The next morning, they went to the Cuihu Church for the Sunday service. On Monday, we sent about a dozen Christians to the Wei house to destroy all the idols. We also hung a cross, the symbol of salvation, there. We worked from morning until noon, not eating or drinking anything. As we left, the father asked how much the charge was, because it is customary to pay for any folk religious activities. We told them that the grace of God is free, just as the prophet Isaiah said: 'Come, all you who are thirsty, come to the waters; and you who have no money, come, buy and eat!' (Isa. 55:1). Within a year, Mulin was a healthy young man. Sometime after Pushi accepted Jesus, suddenly he could walk. After Lin Suiyu accepted Jesus, she asked Christians to pray for her. We fasted and prayed, and she, too, was healed.

Immediately, six neighboring families also wanted to believe in Jesus. The gospel of the kingdom is like yeast (Matt. 13:33). Lord Jesus is the light of this world. Those who follow him will not live in darkness but walk in light. As the true light of God shined upon this family, they escaped their afflictions. The Lord had saved them from darkness and into light, from death to life.

Right now the Wei family enjoys peace. The most precious gift they received was the healing of their hearts by the Lord; the worry, anxiety and insomnia are all gone, replaced by the joy of God, as if they are already living in heaven. In gratitude, they preach the gospel to all who listen. They always tell others, 'I wish I could have heard the gospel sooner – even one day sooner would have been better.' Within a year, the Weis led three families of relatives, a total of 14 people, to Christ.

Within a year of the Wei family conversion, six more families from their village came to Christ, bringing the total to ten. Here are some of their testimonies:

Zhang Qinghai's wife, Yang Sumai, had been sick for four years. Despite spending a great deal of money on many gods and doctors, her condition worsened. Then she heard the gospel and immediately accepted Jesus. Now aged forty-eight, she is totally healed. Every time she comes to worship, she praises the Lord.

The son of Wei Yauxi, Wei Jinjian, aged nineteen, had a mental problem for two years. Medical treatments brought no progress. After he put his faith in Christ, however, he was totally healed and is now a strong and healthy young man. Now Jinjian helps out in all Christian activities, especially the funerals (because we need strong men to be the pallbearers).

Zhen Qingfei, aged forty-two, had not been able to walk for several years, and medical treatment had brought no improvement. He decided that he would sell his son to pay for more medical treatments. Then, less than a month after he committed his life to the Lord, he could walk again. It was a miracle. Now he can work again. The Lord has mercy on the poor and saved this whole family.

Wei Dongbei fell from his roof several years ago. As he was driven to the hospital, there was an accident. Dongbei was very superstitious and did not go to the hospital for treatment. Therefore, both of his legs became paralyzed. After he started to believe in the Lord, however, he was able to walk again with the aid of a crutch.

One day, two of Heng Xin's oxen ate grass poisoned with pesticide. The oxen, white foam coming from their mouths, fell to the ground. There was not even time to call for the veterinarian. Heng Xin called a Christian to kneel down and pray, and immediately the Lord healed his animals.

Yang Zhengju was possessed by evil spirits and was mentally disturbed between the ages of sixteen and twenty-five. During these years, she had been admitted into the mental hospital many times. She had also called upon many deities for help. Yet after she had believed in the Lord for 40 days, she totally recovered.

Chen Jianguo had been possessed by an evil spirit beginning when he was nineteen. During the following 25 years, he would jump around and cause lots of disturbances, sometimes keeping the whole village awake at night. After Chen accepted Christ, however, the evil spirit left him. Every Sunday, Chen goes to church for worship. People in the village are glad now because they can enjoy peace at night.

One day, several evil spirits were trying to possess a man. He ran from his house to the road, with the spirits following him. Meeting a crew of road repairmen, he knew that one of them was a Christian. He asked the Christian for help. The man then noticed that the spirits were no longer chasing him but merely standing at a distance.

The Christian followed this man back to his home. Taking along a few more Christians, he replaced the idols in the man's home with a cross. They prayed for the man and left. That evening the spirits began banging on the man's door, screaming, 'Why did you kick us out?' Curious, the man asked them to explain. They replied, 'We chased you until we saw those spiritual *gongan* [policemen] beside your Christian friend, and we dared not come any nearer. Now you have this cross in your home, and we can't come in. Take it out and let us in!'

The man was so afraid that he didn't sleep the whole night. The next day he went to the church and became a Christian. The spirits have since left him alone.

I don't have time to write out all 60 testimonies of the new Christian families that joined the church in 1996. Further, the reader would not have the patience. Of those who converted, some had heard the gospel for 28 years, others for three years, but most had just heard it. Anyhow, they decided to accept the incarnated God into their lives.

Our coworkers have been busy preaching the gospel in the field. The Holy Spirit often leads us through visions and dreams. As we walk with God, his miracles validate his truth. May all the glory and praise be to the holy name of God.

# Chapter 8

# Remembering the Forgotten

*Over the past two decades, since Deng Xiaoping launched economic reforms, much of China has plunged headlong into the pursuit of money. The relatively wealthy coastal areas have done quite well, as they have more resources to compete in the market. Some regions can build nice schools and hire quality teachers for their children.*

*This economic policy also has victims, however. The remote and rural mountainous areas have been hardest hit. In the past, they could rely on the government to subsidize basic social services – such as education and medical care – for their people. Under the new economic policy, however, local governments must pay for these services themselves. The school administrations in these areas suddenly had to begin levying all kinds of fees, and the poor simply could not afford to send their children to school.*

*One Christian wanted some of the poor children in his small city in southern China to have a decent education. His obedience to Christ has blossomed into a movement that includes many non-Christians. Here is his story.*

Gao Yong's father died when he was very young. His mother, a very devoted Christian, raised him in a small, predominantly Christian village in northern Guangdong. Although the church there was shut down after 1949, Gao and his family still read the Bible at home. In the 1950s, Gao became a teacher.

Like many others, Gao faced many trials during the cultural revolution and had to hide any expression of his faith. Yet he excelled in his profession and was appointed not only as the principal of the best local high school, but also as the educational inspector for the prefecture's education ministry.

In the early 1980s, however, the local church reopened, and Gao began attending. He was invited to join the Communist Party but refused because of his Christian commitment. Instead, he joined the government-sanctioned Democratic Alliance Party, composed mainly of intellectuals.

In 1985, Gao began thinking about the many children who were denied an education because of their poverty. He began asking himself what Jesus would do if he saw these kids on the street. Would he not give them an opportunity for an education? That year, the government ended its education monopoly and began allowing civic groups to run schools. Gao immediately rallied his colleagues in the Democratic Alliance, many of whom were retired teachers. Gao took early retirement from his highly paid job and started the Guangming ('Light' or 'Brightness') Experimental High School – the first nongovernmental school in Guangdong province since 1950.

Gao rented a primary school to use in the evenings and provided all his retired teacher friends with token allowances to serve as volunteers. Tuition was kept low for students from poor backgrounds. The only Christian on the faculty, his love for these young people motivated many retired teachers to join him. Sometimes the school had no electricity, and students had to light candles during class. It operated on a shoestring budget, barely able to pay the token teacher allowances. Still, the rooms were soon packed with students.

Yet Gao knew that there were many more fine young people in the rural areas unable to get an education because of their poverty. To take in those from far-away villages, the school would need to provide not only classrooms but also room and board. Despite the seeming impossibility of all this, Gao believed that God would not forsake these people.

In 1992, a Hong Kong charity heard of his school and donated money for a teaching block. The government also granted a small patch of land next to a garbage dump. The next year, the school had its own campus and immediately converted two classrooms into dormitories and took in some boarding students.

The school also, against much advice to the contrary, and without the necessary resources, took in 19 top-flight students from the impoverished mountain areas, granting them free tuition, room and board for the course of their study over three years. Gao felt that, as a Christian, he simply could not turn these students away. Most of these youths, overjoyed, came with nothing but the clothes they wore. The school appealed to the teachers and other students to donate money to pay for their clothing, food and bedding.

One of the 19, Tang Sanmei, a Yao girl from Liannan county, said, 'My father died a few years ago due to illness; we had no money for the doctor. My mother left my younger brother and me last year, to marry someone else, for it is too poor to stay in this village. I got the top score in the local junior high school and was admitted into senior high school. But how could I afford the tuition? We just lived on handouts from relatives and neighbors. I loved to study, but it was a dream beyond my reach.'

One day, she received a letter from Guangming Experimental High School saying that all her expenses would be paid. The girl cried, knowing that her dream was about to come true. Yet she had no idea how to get the $5 needed to take the bus to Qingyuan, nor did she know how her brother would take care of himself. She knelt in front of her uncle all night, begging for his help.

'My uncle is also very poor,' she said, 'but finally he went out to borrow the money and then put it in my hand. I could not hold back my tears.'

However, after just one term, the school ran out of the money required to keep the 19 students. Sadly, Gao told them that at the end of the term they would have to return home. Their dream of completing high school had been shattered. Alone, he prayed for a miracle.

A couple of days later, Gao learned through his church that a Christian medical team from Hong Kong would be visiting his school to provide check-ups for the students. This would be the first overseas Christian medical team allowed to work in rural Guangdong since 1949. Gao did not talk to any of the medical team members about the 19 students.

However, at the school, one of the team members noticed some girls weeping in the dormitory and learned about the imminent release of the 19 students. The team members felt that they should respond. Returning to Hong Kong, they raised enough money to keep all 19 in school until graduation. This was just the beginning, as the volunteers organized a charity to educationally support underprivileged young people. Since then, these Christians have raised enough money to build a seven-storey dormitory for 240 boarding students – half of whom receive full scholarships. At the entrance of this dormitory, called the Edifice of Love, is an inscription of the apostle Paul's words from 1 Corinthians 13.

Because of Gao's simple faith in God, there is now a well-managed education complex with a high school, a vocational school, a kindergarten and a primary school in Qingyuan City. From the beginning, its objective has been to serve the poor with quality education. Meanwhile, the charity in Hong Kong, inspired by Gao and his Guangming High School, has also built more than a dozen schools in poor, remote rural areas in three provinces in China. Christians and non-Christians alike have been moved by the genuine spirit of charity seen in a simple Christian teacher – Gao Yong – who believes that God cares for the poor and honors his promises.

# Chapter 9

# The Jesus Family

*Since its foundation in the 1920s, the Jesus Family, an indigenous Chinese movement, has tried to build an ideal Christian community modeled on the Jerusalem Church as recorded in the book of Acts. Members share all things and live in self-sufficient rural communities. The Communist Party has had a hard time bringing the Jesus Family under control, for its teaching and practices excelled the Communist ideal. In the early 1950s, the communes were shut down by the government. Yet since their reopening, they have preserved their tradition of sharing and in fact have been growing rapidly in the past two decades. The Jesus Family has been so successful that the government which had once banned the movement praised many of these communities in the early 1980s as model villages.*

*Jesus Family members stress having an intense personal experience with God and, like many believers in China, interpret the Bible allegorically. They also see signs and dreams as important parts of God's continuous revelation, and place strong emphasis on eschatology and divine dispensation.*

*Below are some key events in the life of Dr Feng Lan Xin, who joined this movement in 1941 and later became one of its leaders. He published a total of nine messages in a booklet that has been widely distributed in China. This chapter presents some of these experiences for a wider audience.*

## 1931

Before 1900, my grandfather believed in Christ after reading a gospel tract. Under his leadership, three families in our village accepted the gospel and built a church hall that looked like a farmhouse. My father and my third and fourth uncles all graduated from the Shangdong Tengchow College, paving the way for our generation to have a chance at an education.

After I graduated from the Shoushan High School, operated by the Shangdong Qinzhou Church, I entered the medical college of the Shangdong Christian University, jointly run by various Christian churches in Jinan. During my seven years of medical training, although I had lived in a very nice religious environment, I had no real Christian faith. During holidays, when I returned to my village, I was invited to preach at Sunday worship services. Since I could not refuse, I just preached some messages which I did not believe. I graduated from medical school in 1928 and was invited to practice medicine at the Fuyu Hospital, run by the Zhoucun Church. It was a good job, but I still had not believed in Jesus.

In 1931, the Church of Zhoucun had invited an American pastor, Rev L.C. Osborn from Daming of Hebei province, to preach there for five days. On the afternoon of the last day, I listened to him preach on the theme: 'If one is not reborn, one cannot enter the kingdom of God.' Afterward, touched by this truth, I followed the preacher to his room and asked him if we could pray. As we knelt, I recalled the disrespect I had sometimes exhibited toward my parents and recalled a time when I had stolen some change from my father. I confessed these things to the Lord, and tears began to pour from my eyes. The prayer lasted for less than ten minutes.

I stood up and could feel that my whole being had changed. My heart was filled with joy, and everyone seemed lovable to me. I told the pastor, and he said, 'Thank God; you have been reborn.' I hopped and jumped all the way back to the hospital, which was two kilometers away. I was glad that it was nighttime – no one was on the street to see me. Otherwise, they would have wondered what had happened to me.

In the morning, my heart was still joyful. This joy, however, made me laugh out loud, and I couldn't stop. My laughing got louder and louder. I feared that I might be suffering from schizophrenia. Yet in the midst of my fear, a clear voice in my heart told me: 'Because your soul was saved from hell last night, he is rejoicing in you.' In the past I had believed neither in the existence of the soul nor in hell; therefore, I believed this voice was from the Holy Spirit, who had just begun indwelling my heart. Since this message, I have believed in God, that Jesus is God. I have also believed in heaven and hell and every word of the Bible. Also, I have had peace in my heart, and my behavior has been transformed.

Until this time, I had been well groomed, with nice clothes. To attract the opposite sex, I wore my hair long and always kept a comb in my pocket. (I also wore it this way to cover a depression at the top of my skull.) I decided that God wanted me to address my vanity, so I went to the barber to have a crew cut, despite the objections of the barber. British Christian churches operated our hospital.

In England, no one had crew cuts, other than convicts. When I returned to the hospital, the superintendent gave me a hard time.

Of course, this was not the only change. It became my practice to go to the cafeteria to say grace with the nurses before meals. At home I never let the Bible leave my hand. Every time I ate, I had the Bible next to my bowl, as I read and ate at the same time. Except in very special circumstances, I have always gotten up to pray before dawn, regardless of the season or weather. I have had a loving heart for all Christians, and I am certain that I am part of the body of Christ.

## 1936

In 1935, the Xuan Shen Hui Hospital of Rev Osborn's church in Daming Fu, Hebei province, invited me to work there. The next year, during a morning prayer, a message came into my heart: 'Give thanks for the Church of Jiang Yu Xi Juan.' This message was so clear, it was almost like receiving a telegram.

The village of Jiang Yu Xi Juan was about two kilometers from my home village of Tien Yu Kou, with a small hill in between. I knew of it but had never been there, nor did I know anyone from that village. I certainly did not know if there were any Christians. After hearing God's message in Daming Fu, I didn't do anything in particular except to give thanks for Jiang Yu Xi Juan's Church in my daily prayer.

At that time, the doctors in our hospital had an annual one-month holiday. During mine, back in my home at Shangdong, I asked my father, 'How many Christians are there in Jiang Yu Xi Juan?'

He replied, 'Not a single soul.'

I reasoned that if there were no Christians, there could not be a church; therefore, I would go there myself and evangelize the village. I told my father.

'No need to go there, for no one will believe,' he replied. 'In our village there have been only three families of Christians in 30 years.' Then I told my father of the message I had received from the Lord in Daming Fu. That afternoon, I traveled to Jiang Yu Xi Juan by myself.

After I arrived, knowing no one, I stood on the main street and began singing songs of Jesus, including 'There is only one true God and he is the God of heaven.' At first, children gathered around me while I sang; later, some adults began to come. I told them about my message from the Lord at Daming Fu. I also told them about the benefits of believing in Jesus, sharing the changes that had taken place in me.

That moment, a man named Du Zheng Fu, who had been listening with his son and daughter-in-law, suddenly said, 'Sir, can you please come to our house?' I followed him to his home. As they served me tea, I kept on speaking about the goodness of the gospel.

As I left them that evening, I said, 'I can't stay at Tien Yu Kou for too long. In a few days, I will be at my father-in-law's place – in Qu Jia Juan – for a while. And then I will return to Daming Fu.'

After I had been in Qu Jia Juan for three days, a neighbor told me, 'There are two people from Jiang Yu Xi Juan looking for you.' I thought they must have been patients looking for a doctor. To my surprise, I saw that one of them was Du Zheng Fu, who had invited me to his home. The other was a Mr Zhang. They said, 'We have come to tell you that both of us have accepted Jesus.' Every week, following their conversion, they would climb the hilly road two kilometers to Tien Yu Kou for Sunday services.

There was a man named Zhang Jiao You. He greatly respected his widowed mother but had been a compulsive gambler for ten years. The family had no peace, and he was very sad. He had heard that those who joined 'the Jesus religion' did not gamble. He found Brother Zhang, who by this time had been a Christian for just a year, and asked him, 'Uncle, would Jesus take me if I believe?'

'Of course you are welcome,' Brother Zhang replied. 'Jesus will take anyone.'

Zhang Jiao You immediately said, 'I believe in Jesus.' He then joined Du and Zhang for Sunday worship at Tien Yu Kou Church. Zhang Jiao You has not gambled in the many decades since, and is a changed man.

In 1937, dozens of families in that village converted to Christianity. We selected those who had sufficient Christian knowledge for baptism. Seventy people were baptized at the first baptismal service. The daily morning and evening meeting at the Jiang Xi Yu Juan Church has continued uninterrupted for 50 years. Not only does this church have a lot of believers, it has been richly blessed with many graces, including visions of heaven and hell.

One day the aged mother of Zhang Jiao You, the former gambler, became very sick and had to stay in bed. For three days she couldn't eat, drink, speak, or go to the bathroom. Because she was old, someone stayed beside her at all times. On the third day, the old lady opened her eyes and said, 'I am fine. Heaven is a good place. Those of you who have not yet believed in Jesus must believe in him quickly. Those who have already believed must believe with a fervent heart. The heavenly Father told me to come back, and I said to him, "Heavenly Father, I don't want to go back," but he told me that there are still some things for me to do; he will take me a year later.'

The old lady recuperated very well. She counted her days – one month, two months, three months, six months, and so on – until exactly one year since her recovery had elapsed. At her request, her son invited all the Christians of the village over to their house. Wearing white clothing and a white hat, with crosses on them, she rested on her bed. As the others talked elsewhere in the house, she died peacefully.

In 1942, Chang Jian You, a middle-class peasant, was the first person in the church to sell all his farmland and properties and give them to the poor. Later, Du Jin Jie (the second son of the first believer, Mr Du), and then Niu Hua Yi, followed his example. Liu Hong Shen and a few others also sold their properties.

Through the guidance of the Holy Spirit, by faith they built a large church hall two-thirds of a kilometer west of Xi Juan Zhuang. They also built several dozen houses and started living together as a family, sharing all goods, and working for the Lord. This lasted until 1951, when, for a variety of reasons, they were split up, and the former ecclesial situation was restored (the church returned to the former unified church). Since the beginning God has been very merciful to this church.

The Lord had told me to give thanks for this faith community even before its existence. The Lord has richly blessed this Juang Yu Xi Juan Church and proven the trustworthiness of his own word.


# 1941


There were five churches in or near my home village. Four of them, including the one in Tien Yu Kou, had church halls. However, the one in Da Yu Cun, four kilometers northwest of ours, did not. For many decades, the Christians of this village gathered at Elder Wang Jiu Shu's home for worship.

Every morning, I prayed for these places individually. One day, the Lord gave me a message: 'I will give the Da Yu Cun Church a church hall.'

In my prayer, I repeatedly said, 'Lord, are you going to give Da Yu Cun Church a church hall?' Each time I repeated this question, my heart was moved and I began to shed tears. From then on, whenever I prayed for this place in my morning prayers, I would cry. This continued for six or seven days. It finally began to sink in that God would indeed build a church hall for the Da Yu Cun Church.

The next Sunday, I traveled ten kilometers from Qu Jia Juan to Da Yu Cun to join their Sunday services. Several dozen people were there. I preached to them about offerings, loving God, and his desire to give them a church hall. Then we prayed together, and I cried as before.

After the service, I invited them to sit down and discuss this issue with me. The region had suffered a three-year drought; many people had died from the famine. The Christians told me they even had to line up for a long time near the well to secure drinking water. Certainly there would be insufficient water for any construction work. Every family in that village was very poor; not one owned even a cow. Any building materials would have to be hauled from the other side of the river – and the hauling required a cow. I said, 'Let us pray.' As I prayed, the Lord kept telling me, 'I will give Da Yu Cun Church a church hall.' At last I told these friends, 'I have to leave.'

Several days after my visit to that village, some Christians from Da Yu Cun came to Qu Jia Juan looking for me and said, 'All the problems we discussed have been solved. There is a spring at the southern tip of the village that can provide water for the construction of a mud wall. We have also borrowed a cow to haul the quarry.' Rejoicing, I went to Nan Xian preaching the gospel.

About twenty days later, I returned to Qu Jia Juan. A sentry ordered me to identify myself and state my business. Once I did, he replied, 'Our captain instructed me that if you passed by here he would like to meet you.' Having no choice, I met the captain. He was very nice and gave me $200 in cash as I was leaving, even though I tried to refuse it. So I took it along.

When I came back to Qu Jia Juan, Christians from Da Yu Cun Church told me that the four houses of the church hall had been completed. As they were building the church hall, many people came and offered money or goods. The construction project went very smoothly. I asked whether they still owed any money. They said they were still lacking $200. I gave them the $200, and the hall was completed.

The smooth completion of the Da Yu Cun church hall, especially under very difficult circumstances, clearly shows the power of God. If we act in accordance to his will, God will be with us to strengthen us and to prepare ways for us.

# Chapter 10

# A Persevering Pastor

*Tongchuan is about one hundred and twenty kilometers north of Xi'an, China's ancient capital. Since the 1950s, the main industry has been a copper mine. Cave homes are unique to northwestern China. Villagers in Tongchuan live in these dwellings, which are carved into both sides of the main slope. At the top of one slope is a large complex of several buildings, with a big cross at the top. This is the Tongchuan Christian Church, which averages 2,000 people in attendance every Sunday and has 30 smaller churches (or gathering points) scattered in town. Total church membership is now 15,000, compared to 20 when it started in 1950. Below is the story of Zhu Chengxin, who founded the church about fifty years ago.*

During the anti-Western Boxer Rebellion of 1900, many missionaries and Chinese Christians were slaughtered, often at the behest of the ruling Qing Dynasty. Among the hardest hit was the Christian community in Shangdong. Many of the families there fled to neighboring provinces, such as Shaanxi, and established new settlements, some of which were given Christian names. Many of these villages still exist today, although the government has given them names

with socialist themes. The local people, however, still refer
to them by their old Christian names. Zhu Chengxin was
born into a Christian family in Gospel village, in Sanyuan
county, near Xi'an.

In the late 1940s, Zhu felt called to full-time ministry
and studied at Shanghai's Christian Spiritual Institute. Many
of the students there sought a deep relationship with God
through prayer and Scripture reading. Normally, students
from the graduating class would seek the Lord's guidance
on future ministry via long periods of fasting and prayer.
Many of the young people received visions to go to the
frontier areas, such as Xinjiang and Yunnan, to do pioneer
mission work among the minority peoples. Most chose to
do the work 'by faith,' meaning that they would not join a
formal mission board and instead would just go, trusting
God to provide.

Zhu, like other classmates, earnestly sought the Lord's
guidance. After a week of prayer, however, he had received
no visions. In one of the morning chapels, however, he heard
about the ministry of three Bible women at a place called
Keshi, in the extreme northwestern tip of China, near the
USSR and Afghanistan. These women were praying for a
young man to join them. Zhu prayed about it and wrote
them a letter, asking to join them. Receiving a positive reply,
he began his journey. But the civil war between the Communists and some of the Nationalist factions was not over.
Martial law had been imposed, and all travel had to be
approved by the local cadres.

On the way to Keshi, Zhu went to Lanzhou, where he
hoped to catch a bus to Urumqi. Unfortunately, security
agents from Xi'an were following him, believing that a
young man would only travel to the middle of nowhere
because he was a spy working for the Nationalists. Boarding
the bus, he was arrested and interrogated for many days.

The police simply could not believe that he was a missionary seeking to serve in Xinjiang, living by faith. Zhu neither confessed to his alleged crime nor informed on his colleagues. Eventually, the Lanzhou police escorted him to Xi'an, handing him over to the Public Security Bureau. Later, the authorities discovered that Zhu indeed was a Bible school graduate from Shaanxi, as he had said. He was finally sent back to the Shaanxi Christian Church. He returned to his home village, looking for a parish to serve.

At that time, the political climate was not favorable toward Christians. The church – having had a long relationship with Western missionaries and mission boards – was under tremendous pressure to denounce the West. Zhu, who had no connections with missionaries, was allowed to serve at a very small church in Tongchuan, which was merely a preaching station with a small hut with a leaking roof. Zhu lived in the church and began to minister to the 20 believers there. Because of intense socialist propaganda from the government, most churches in China suffered drastic membership declines. Yet the Tongchuan Church started to grow, reaching more than one hundred members by the end of the decade.

Starting in 1958, the government selected several regions to launch a 'socialist reeducation campaign,' as part of the so-called Great Leap Forward. Some cadres even tried to eradicate religion by force, making everyone work in factories or farms – even pastors. Zhu worked as a carpenter. In 1960, the cadres at Tongchuan suspended church services and held daily political meetings there instead, which all Christians were required to attend. During these meetings, the Christians were pressured to denounce their faith and accuse Zhu of being 'a parasite of the people.' Those who cooperated would be rewarded. In only a few days, some of the believers openly renounced their faith and were publicly praised by the government. Some concocted stories to implicate Zhu, while many openly denounced him in the church. After nearly one hundred days of continuous meetings, only eight people still confessed their faith. More than one hundred people – members of his flock whom Zhu had ministered to for almost a decade – left the church after publicly humiliating him. Yet throughout, Zhu never defended himself; he simply remained silent as the wild accusations flew.

This effectively killed the church. Zhu, however, continued to hold family worship services at his home, while the government declared victory in its war against religion. A year later, however, grasping the damage it had wrought, the authorities began relaxing the policy. Very soon, Christians began returning, with their apologies, to Zhu, who refused to hold a grudge. He took them in without saying a word. By 1964, his church again had more than one hundred people worshiping every Sunday. But in 1965, the church was officially closed when the local government launched a political campaign against all 'capitalist poison,' including religion. The next year, at the start of the cultural revolution, virtually every church building in China was confiscated, including the small one in Tongchuan.

Meanwhile, Zhu was becoming a rather famous carpenter, specializing in dowry chests. Zhu took pride in his work, and many government officials became his friends after he made furniture for them. As the political climate began to relax in the early 1970s, Zhu started holding secret worship services in his home. If caught, he could be convicted of a serious crime. By 1976, several dozen people were gathering there. The local cadres, perhaps sensing that change was in the air, tolerated this open secret.

In the early 1980s, the government formally allowed freedom of religious belief and permitted churches to reopen. Immediately, Zhu's congregation grew to several hundred, so he donated his house for the building, placing oil-paper over the courtyard so that more people could attend. At first, the government refused to allow Zhu's church to be registered. Later, however, a kind official courageously gave official approval. The Tongchuan Church, however, was a source of embarrassment, because it was growing faster than the local Communist Party.

By the end of the decade, the church had several thousand believers and many gathering points in the surrounding towns and villages. Under Zhu's leadership, the church organized teams of volunteers to serve the community regularly: barber teams offering free haircuts, doctors offering free medical consultations, electricians providing free repairs of electric appliances. Whenever there was a natural disaster in surrounding areas, the church contributed to relief efforts.

Before long, Christians were being praised as good citizens, and the church was named a Model Civilized Unit – an honor conferred on organizations demonstrating high moral values. The government even invited Zhu to be a member of the Tongchuan Municipal Political Consultative Conference, a political body representing different social groups to the government. Zhu's church had become such an important organization that it could not be ignored. When the church needed to expand its buildings, the city government allowed it to rent the municipal theater – the largest hall in the city – to hold Sunday service for a whole year. This is almost unheard of in other areas, since religious activities can normally only be held in designated religious venues.

By the end of 1999, Tongchuan Church had more than fifteen thousand members and 30 registered daughter churches or meeting points. There were also many nonregistered gathering points. The church also built a training center, which can house several dozen students, and runs a semiannual three-month training program for lay preachers. With a staff of several pastors, it is the major Christian hub for the whole northern part of Shaanxi province.

Although Zhu is already beyond retirement age, he splits his time between Tongchuan Church, as senior minister, and the Xi'an Theological School, as vice-president and faculty member. Two of his sons are now pastors serving elsewhere – to continue their persevering father's work.

# Chapter 11

# Gospel Connections

*People sometimes wonder why so many Christian communities have developed in remote villages in China in recent years. These places are often in the middle of nowhere, with no previous exposure to Christianity. Indeed, unlike some active evangelistic efforts by local Christian communities, many of these new communities grow without any contact from churches in the region. Also, they are far from cities or ports where Christians from overseas might come to share the gospel, and they often lack overseas contacts. The following living example of such a Christian community illustrates this church growth phenomenon in China.*

The Qingyuan prefecture lies at the northern tip of Guang-dong province. With eight counties, it is one of the poorest regions in Guangdong. Although missionaries arrived over a hundred years ago, Christianity made little progress among the inhabitants, who were mostly farmers. By 1949, there were several churches, with perhaps a few hundred followers. Soon, however, with the ascension to power of the Communists, the churches were closed. There was no public Christian activity until the early 1980s. Some of the counties had no Christians at all. Yangshan county, just north of the prefecture seat, had no record of any Christian presence before 1990.

In 1991, a retired primary school teacher, Chen Shaoying, visited her daughter, who was having minor surgery, at the county hospital. The Chens live in a small town named Cigong, about 30 kilometers from Yangshan, the county seat. In the hospital, the Chens became friends with a patient who came from another small town. One day, a distant relative of this person, who happened to be a Christian, came to visit. The relative offered to pray for the young lady. Chen had not experienced Christianity before, having been told that it was an imperialistic attack on China. Curious, she asked the relative to explain this religion.

Hearing the gospel for the first time, Chen and her daughter accepted Jesus Christ as their Savior. A few days later, they returned to Cigong, and Chen immediately began sharing this new faith with her friends, neighbors, and relatives; however, the response was only modest. By the end of the year, seven people had made commitments to Christ. Chen began holding small gatherings at her home. She also traveled to Qingyuan city, the prefecture seat, looking for Christians who could help her. Making contact with the church there, Chen returned with a Bible and some booklets on basic Christian doctrine.

Most of the people in that region believe in traditional Chinese folk religions, which are corruptions of Buddhism and Taoism. They will worship any god as long as it 'works.' Not surprisingly, people began asking Chen to pray to this 'new' God named Jesus on their behalf. Several experienced physical healing, and word spread that Chen's God was a powerful deity able to perform miracles. Many people, attracted by the power of God, became followers of Jesus. Their ranks grew to 70 by the end of 1992, and more than one hundred and fifty in 1993, and they held meetings in five different homes.

Getting wind of this new 'cult', the local government tried to stop it by administrative means. The man in charge of religious affairs in the county was an army veteran, a former political commissar strongly opposed to religion. He told Chen to disband the groups or he would throw the Christians in jail.

Seeking help from the Qingyuan Church, Chen discovered that her group could exercise its right to religious belief under the Constitution if it registered. However, when Chen spoke again with the antagonistic cadre, he said, 'Since there has never been Christianity in this county, we will not allow a Christian group to register here. You will get registered over my dead body. Now get out, or I'll arrest you.'

As in this case, local cadres often disregard national law. Despite the continuous intervention of the prefecture's Religious Affairs Bureau and the Christian Council, the local government refused to budge. The government said there had to be a certain number of religious believers before a church could register. Then the number Chen provided was not accepted, since none of the 'so-called' Christians in Cigong had been baptized. Next, when Madam Chen suggested that the government invite an ordained minister to baptize the believers, the government replied that because there was no church in Cigong, there was no one qualified to invite a pastor. To top it off, there wasn't any ordained minister in Qingyuan anyway; all the sacraments had to be conducted by ordained ministers invited from Guangzhou, the provincial capital. Finally, the local government warned that any pastor who came there illegally would be arrested. This kind of catch-22 is, in fact, very common for new Christian communities in China, which are largely at the mercy of the government. Chen and her group were forced into hiding for two years.

In 1994, at least two hundred and fifty believers in Cigong were secretly gathering in different homes. The local government often harassed Chen and the other believers, threatening arrest. During their many confrontations, Madam Chen simply said, 'Go ahead and arrest me.' In fact, she had already packed a small bag and was ready to go to jail at any time.

In spite of all this, the Christian community kept growing, spreading even beyond Cigong. That same year, Hsu Shuicun, a nurse at the Yangshan People's Hospital, visited her mother in Cigong. Hsu's marriage was in trouble, as her husband was having an affair. She had no peace and was seeking advice from fortunetellers.

One day she visited her aunt, hoping to have her palms read. However, a neighbor, Mrs Leung, told Hsu that there was no need to read palms, because she knew of a more powerful deity who could help people. Coming to her house, Hsu saw a calendar with a cross on it and recognized it as a symbol of Christianity. Her high school teacher had warned her that Christianity was a foreign, imperialistic religion. Thus, she found it very strange to discover this religion in a rural place like Cigong.

Mrs Leung shared her testimony with Hsu, who immediately accepted the gospel. Hsu took a Bible, which had several pages missing, back home with her to Yangshan. She shared her new faith with her mother-in-law and she, too, accepted this God. Soon, Hsu spent most of her spare time studying the Bible and sharing her faith. Many nurses and doctors have now accepted the gospel at the hospital where she works. Hsu travels to Cigong to seek instruction in the faith from Madam Chen, and she has started her own family gatherings.

Currently, there are more than five hundred Christians at Yangshan, and they are now seeking registration. They use the local cement factory's hall for Sunday services, and they plan to build their own church. Although the gospel did not save Hsu's marriage – she and her husband divorced a year later – Hsu experiences peace and consolation from God and is a very dedicated lay preacher.

Besides Yangshan, the gospel has traveled to towns and villages near Cigong via Christians with relatives in those places. Meanwhile, Chen tried to get the Cigong Church officially established. Discussing the problem with the church leaders in Qingyuan, they came up with a two-pronged approach.

In 1995, the Qingyuan Church invited Rev Kim-kwong Chan from Hong Kong to hold a baptismal service. The Christians of Cigong and Yangshan rented a bus to transport 60 Christians to Qingyuan Church. Following the service, Cigong had 40 officially initiated Christians, Yangshan had 20. The 40 were now eligible to apply for registration at the Cigong Christian gathering point. At the same time, the Qingyuan Church held a three-week lay preacher training program. Chen and several others completed this program and are now certified to be officially recognized lay preachers – another criterion for registration.

Meanwhile, the prefecture Religious Affairs Bureau and the Christian Council of Qingyuan jointly issued a letter of complaint to the Qingyuan People's Congress against the cadres in charge of religious affairs of Yangshan county. The letter charged that they insulted the Christian religion, created problems among the people, and refused to implement the national policy of freedom of religious belief. The leader was forced into early retirement and replaced with cadres more sympathetic toward religion. These new cadres gave oral approval for Christians in both Cigong and Yangshan to hold meetings and allowed them to apply for registration.

Both communities grew rapidly, with many people experiencing healing after believing the gospel. By this time, Chen and her coworkers didn't need to travel to the nearby villages to preach, because many believers would bring their seeking friends and relatives to Chen's house for prayer or discussions about the faith. Chen also made sure the Christians visited the old people's hostel and shared their resources with the poor.

The Christians in Cigong and Yangshan earned respect in their communities despite their lack of registration. Those in Cigong rented a house for their Sunday worship services, which now have several hundred people attending every week. On 28 December 1998, the local government finally granted them the official registration as a 'Protestant temporary meeting point,' with the serial number 001 – the first such registration in the whole county. By then, the church had several baptized members, a team of four lay preachers and two more applying for seminary training.

Meanwhile, the Yangshan community, which numbers several hundred believers, is currently without an official registration. Both communities are now planning to build their own churches with help from Christians in Hong Kong.

Only ten years ago, there was not a single Christian in the county. Now there are more than one thousand baptized members in two large communities and many smaller gatherings. It all began with a retired teacher who visited her daughter in a county hospital.

# Chapter 12

# 'A Weak Limb'

*Christianity has experienced several intense nation-wide persecutions in China. By the end of the nineteenth century, the Chinese in general had become virulently anti-Western. At the time, the Western nations were expanding their commercial and political interests by force, and the Chinese government – the Qing Dynasty – was in no position to resist. The once proud Middle Kingdom was humiliated.*

*Along with the Western soldiers and merchants came the missionaries. Chinese Christians were therefore regarded as traitors, accused of serving the foreigners over the Chinese national interest. This long-suppressed anger among the Chinese suddenly erupted, as the government endorsed a kind of grass-roots folk religious movement called the Boxer Rebellion. The Boxers claimed that they were invincible, protected by the Chinese deities, and able to defeat the foreigners, who had modern weapons. Many foreigners, including hundreds of missionaries, were killed by the mobs.*

*To protect the expatriates, the Foreign Coalition Force invaded China. However, in an ugly display of raw power, it robbed Beijing of several centuries' worth of national treasures, burning much that couldn't be carried away. The national humiliation continued until 1949, when the Chinese Communist Party declared the nation free of Western influence. The long-standing suspicion toward Christianity by Chinese authorities is partly a result of this national history.*

*The Boxers also massacred tens of thousands of Chinese Christians, forcing many to flee their homes. Would such persecution discourage people from receiving the gospel? Would the victims still trust this God, introduced by foreigners, who seemed to bring them bad luck? The following testimony, written by a seventy-six-year-old lay preacher named Zheng Deguang from Hebei province, may provide the answer. It reveals how Chinese Christians interpret history – especially disasters and calamities – from the perspective of their Christian faith.*

When the Boxers killed my Grandma, she was thirty-eight years of age. In fact, they killed six of our Christian family of eight on the same day. Only my uncle, who was fifteen, and my mother, who was nine, were spared. They had a hard time surviving. My uncle escaped to the Christian church at Fangshuo county in Inner Mongolia. My mother was sold to the Li family for 20 silver dollars to pay the family debts – probably brought on by the funeral.

When my mother was seventeen, she was made to marry my father, Zheng Piru. During the farming season, he worked in the fields; after the harvest, he worked as a blacksmith. He labored very hard to feed a family of 18, including his parents and siblings.

I was born in June 1924. My grandmother worshiped the idols, and our family faced a succession of calamities from the devil's hand. From 1926 to 1927, my grandfather died, my father died, my second uncle died, my second aunt remarried and took the two children with her, my third uncle died, and my third aunt remarried and took her daughter with her. My third elder sister and fourth younger sister also died. Within a year, we lost 11 family members. Furthermore, my eldest brother and I were both critically ill. Our family didn't have enough to eat; we had no warm clothing. We were struggling to survive, and we were desperate.

While our family was in the midst of crisis, my long-lost uncle (who was now forty-eight) returned, looking for his sister – my mother. When he finally found my mother, he did not recognize her until they compared their family histories. They recounted all the suffering they had experienced over the previous 33 years, a seemingly endless tale of sadness. Then my uncle shared the gospel with us, and the whole family received Jesus. Three days later, my brother and I were completely well. In August of that year, we went with my uncle to live in Fangshuo county, Inner Mongolia, 240 kilometers from our home village.

In 1933, when I was nine, our whole family received baptism. By the blessing of God, we had sufficient food and were all healthy. My boyish faith was very shallow, however. There was no money to send me to school, so I had no education and was unable to read the Bible.

In 1938, when I was fifteen, the Communists came looking for draftees. If a family had three brothers, one had to join. Since my oldest brother was the breadwinner and the middle brother had gone for an apprenticeship, I was drafted into the army, where I received an atheistic education. In 1942, I was captured by the Japanese Military Police and charged as a spy. Jailed for 72 days, I was tortured seven times. A few minutes before my scheduled execution, God moved the hearts of my cellmates, and 62 of them pleaded with the Japanese to release me. My life was spared.

In 1948, the Chinese Nationalist Party captured me and sentenced me to life in prison. However, I was released by the victorious Communist Party in 1949. I worked for the government and the Party for the next 17 years. I worked as a manager for a foundry. I also received the following appointments: people's deputy of Guisui city, Suiyuan province (later merged into Hebei province), chairman of the city steel workers' union, jury of the city court, and president of the city's drama troupe.

But in October 1967, during the cultural revolution, I was classified as an 'antirevolutionary element'. I faced what was called 'struggle sessions' every three or four days. During these days, I was denied water. I developed a throat problem and was under medical treatment from 1968 to 1969. In June 1969, I was diagnosed with terminal cancer of the esophagus, and I made preparations for my funeral. I soon became unable to drink any water, my life sustained by intravenous transfusions. My weight dropped from 150 pounds to 75 pounds. I couldn't speak and became very agitated whenever I heard noises.

On 1 July 1969, at 1.20 a.m., I cried out to God, saying, 'Oh Lord, when I was young I had the grace to be baptized in your name. Later on, I was weak and received education in atheism. During the past 30 years, I have lived like the prodigal son, far away from the Father. Give me ten times more physical suffering. Just don't send my soul to hell. I am willing to endure this pain, even if my flesh is rotting away.'

At 8.30 a.m. the following morning, I found that I could eat the food. Suddenly, I felt good, and the illness in my body was gone. More than thirty years later, I am still working for the Lord.

When I was younger, I had left his path in search of worldly goods. I smoked, drank, and sought earthly comforts. I sinned, and the sin just trapped me. Its burden pressed heavily on my heart. The further away I went from God, the more sufferings I had from the devil, and the more sins I committed against God.

But in the darkest moment of my life, I thought of Jesus and cried out to him in real repentance. In mercy and grace, he forgave all my sins and healed my body. I determined to serve him and work hard for him. In the time since, I have learned more about God and prayed more to God. As a lay preacher, I used to read the Bible and lead meetings. However, now that I am older I can't do as many things for the Lord, but I can still pray. I am a weak limb in the body of Christ.

# Conclusion

When foreign missionaries were expelled from China in the mid-1950s, many missiologists suggested that the church, which numbered one million in 1949, would cease to exist without its umbilical cord to the West. The church was reduced to a tiny voice simply echoing the political views of the Communist government. Dissenters were jailed or sent to labor camps. Some theologians in the West romantically called the cultural revolution, when virtually all visible forms of Christianity ceased to exist in China, the *missio Dei*, in which a new humanity was being formed via Chairman Mao.

In the late 1970s, Christianity was once again allowed to exist under government control. Most observers believed that Christianity would remain a tiny minority. After three decades of atheistic education, a decade of total disappearance, prolonged government restriction, and virtually total isolation from the worldwide Christian community, its prospects could not be considered bright.

Yet despite all these unfavorable factors, the church exhibited the power of the living Christ. In 1982, the government estimated the Christian population at three million, and, in 1989, ten million. More accurate statistics have suggested that there are at least twenty-five million

Christians in China. During the past decade, many mission agencies, encouraged by the reopening of China and the reemergence of the Chinese Christian community, have made plans to make the country a missiological priority.

To be honest, we must ask: does the Chinese church need foreign missionaries? Hasn't it done better without them? With the seemingly miraculous resurrection of the Chinese church, what should mission agencies do now?

Before 1949, there were at least one hundred and fifty different denominations represented by various mission boards in China. After 1949, the government established the 'Three-Self Patriotic Movement' (TSPM) for the church, calling for self-administration, self-support, and self-propagation. Theologically, this meant the church was to be run by Chinese rather than by foreigners; politically, the movement was a symbol of nationalism and patriotism; missiologically, it declared the end of foreign mission in China. When the Three-Self Patriotic Movement came on the scene, the church entered a post-denominational era with one officially recognized church, without any denominational ties to the universal church.

Most of the Christian growth in recent years has occurred in the rural areas without any previous Christian presence. These 'house church' communities often meet in households and hardly resemble other ecclesiastical forms in the West. Further, the larger autonomous Christian communities adopted a form of church life somewhat similar to the early church. These contextually developed church forms are unique to the Chinese church and well rooted in its sociopolitical settings. Can a foreign missionary contribute in such a context? Only if one believes that other denominational traditions – developed from their own historical and social backgrounds – are superior or more 'biblical' than what has emerged in China.

Despite its growth, the church is still a tiny minority among China's 1.3 billion people. It has been linked to the introduction of Christianity in the nineteenth century, when the Chinese nation was humiliated by Western powers. Further, it is under the strict control of the government and the Chinese Communist Party and exists totally at the mercy of the local Chinese Communist Party cadres. Socially, it is restricted within the walls of church buildings. It cannot run schools or participate in the country's civil life, such as in marriage or education. It is confined within a tightly bound policy and is constantly monitored. Most of its members have little money or status. Most of its national and provincial leaders are elderly, vetted by the government because of their loyalty to the state rather than to the church. Most of the churches are run by laity with little theological training. Many churches in China live in isolation, with limited access to other Christian groups, much less to foreign counterparts. In short, the Chinese church lacks wealth, sociopolitical status, social influence, trained workers, access to information, and educated laity.

Yet this church has humbled many missiologists and ecclesiologists. It has grown between ten and twenty times during the past few decades – an accomplishment that challenges most contemporary mission and church growth theories. It seems that the Chinese church can manage without many current mission requirements – funding, trained experts, paid staff, social services, outreach stations, sophisticated programs and strategies, favorable social and political conditions, political influence, international support, concentrated media exposure, coordinated activities and public evangelistic rallies. It seems to come down on the most fundamental question in missiology – mission of God or mission of man, power of God or strength of man – firmly on the side of the former. Like the mustard seed or the yeast, the seemingly smallest and weakest can grow into the largest. The power of powerlessness is a familiar biblical paradox, as illustrated by the cross. Perhaps the Chinese church can inspire us toward new thinking in mission. Is it time to call for a missions moratorium in China, seeing how well the local church has done without missionary effort?

Still, we are all part of the universal church. Local and national churches are all part of the larger body of Christ. Each part contributes in its own way to the well-being of the rest. There are, in fact, many areas that the larger church can share with the Chinese church. At the same time, the Chinese church can enrich the spirituality of the non-Chinese Christian community. The Chinese church has had a unique pilgrimage, through the valley of the shadow of death, and has emerged as a vibrant community with little to rely on except the faithfulness of God. The Western church, by contrast, has faced secularism, the peace movement, technological advancements, liberation theology, feminist theology, ecotheology and so on. Both have much to share with the other. The Chinese church can 're-evangelize' other churches by helping them focus on ecclesiastical simplicity, whereas the Western church can share its sophistication in theology and church life.

Despite its significant achievements, the Chinese church still faces many challenges and would benefit from outside help. Most of its members and lay leaders need training. Without a better grasp of basic Christian doctrine, more and more Christian groups will go astray and become cults and sects – a major problem in the Chinese church. Its seminaries need to be expanded and upgraded.

The church in China faces critical shortages of pastors, trained laity, and literature – in short, of teaching and teaching resources. Overseas groups can help address these teaching shortages by sharing their resources. However, this is a sensitive area because it touches upon the gray area of the official policy prohibiting foreign mission work in China. Such help must be done under the jurisdiction of the church. It has to be relevant to the issues facing the Chinese church.

Further, Western denominationalism is contrary to the current post-denominational church reality in China. The former patronizing attitude is no longer welcomed or tolerated. Western helpers must also find a balance between the leaders of the autonomous Christian communities and the officially endorsed representatives of the church.

There is another area where foreign Christian groups may help the Chinese church. The government, though atheistic, is taking a pragmatic approach to religion. Religious groups are allowed to exist as long as they can make concrete contributions to society. The government is seeking to eradicate poverty in China, where more than sixty million people still earn less than $60 annually. Since the early 1990s, it has officially allowed the church to channel resources, even foreign ones, for charity and social services.

For a long time, the church was accused of being un-patriotic and otherworldly. Now it can consolidate its position in Chinese society and establish a positive social image. But again, this must be done with great caution. The government is by no means opening the door for foreign groups to operate charities. However, it may open doors for new forms of mission. What is called for is a missiology of servanthood. We need interchurch cooperation based on the spirit of equality and partnership, mission partners rather than missionaries, social projects with a Christian spirit rather than church projects within the ecclesiastical community, silent witness like the parable of the yeast rather than the vocal proclamation of the gospel in the marketplace.

There are, indeed, many new forms of possible ministry for overseas Christians to share the message of Christ while working with Christians in China. As China continues to open up, we may anticipate a new category of unconventional mission projects. Chinese authorities are open to agencies of goodwill which will work as equal partners to alleviate poverty in the rural communities, especially among the national minorities, who inhabit the most difficult terrain in the country.

Foreign missionaries, starting with the Nestorians from Syria, have been in China since the seventh century, followed by the Franciscans in the twelfth century, the Jesuits in the sixteenth century, and by the various Protestant groups during the past two centuries. Today there is little room for foreign Christians who emphasize their denominational distinctives at the expense of the faith shared by all Christians. There is no room for those who disrespect the local culture, who deprive Chinese Christians of their dignity and who deny their cultural heritage. Nor is there room for those who create disunity among Christians. However, there is room for those who come with humble spirit to learn about what God has done among his people in China, and who appreciate the local culture, customs and norms. There is room for those who witness to the love of God through their deeds above their words. There is certainly room for those who serve with Chinese Christians as equal partners.

China remains the largest political entity largely unreached by the gospel. With thirty to forty million Muslims, perhaps five million Tibetans, and a government hostile to religion in general and Christianity in particular, it is one of the greatest challenges of our generation for mission-minded Christians. China is opening to the outside world, and the church there is struggling to establish a genuine local expression. If we can share the Chinese church's pain and burdens now, we may, when Christ becomes the soul of this great nation, share her joy and glory.

# Appendix 1

# Dissenting Voices

Christian communities are divided into two camps in China. The first, part of the officially sanctioned Three-Self Patriotic Movement, submits to government registration and a certain degree of monitoring and control. In exchange, Three-Self churches can openly engage in ecclesiastical activities, such as printing the Bible and operating seminaries. The amount of freedom they can exercise depends on the current political atmosphere as well as the local government cadres' attitude toward religion. The latter can range from support to suppression.

The second camp holds that the church cannot submit to any secular administration, since Jesus Christ, not Caesar, is her head. The activities of this unregistered 'house church' movement are, technically speaking, illegal. These churches often experience various levels of harassment and persecution. The government's policy toward them ranges from toleration to eradication.

While Christians in the West often simplistically categorize the spirituality of Chinese Christians according to whether they are in the official or underground factions, the reality is complex, with a vast gray area. Among the nonregistered groups are all types of theological persuasions, from fundamentalist to hypercharismatic. Many pseudo-Christian groups, including extreme sects or cults, are also part of the underground faction. Within the officially recognized community, meanwhile, are views ranging from full support of Communist teaching to a pragmatic use of official status to gain the opportunity for ministry, even cooperating with nonregistered groups.

Amid the rapid changes occurring in society, the church in China is still searching for her identity. More than twenty Bible and theological schools are operated by the China Christian Council, the official Protestant organization. The CCC upholds the old 1930s Three-Self slogan (Self-Administer, Self-Support, and Self-Propagate) as a guiding principle for churches. This principle, adopted in 1950, is more of a political reaction to the foreign missionary domination of the Chinese church prior to 1949 than a theological position. Although it calls for the autonomy of the Chinese church from foreign control, it does not advocate independence from the Chinese government nor the Chinese Communist Party. All of the CCC schools supposedly train Protestant ministers who support the regime and accept the Three-Self principle.

The top theological school in China is Nanjing Union Theological Seminary, which runs a four-year undergraduate program and a three-year graduate program, equivalent to the Master of Divinity (MDiv) degree. This school trains the leaders and theologians of the Chinese church. Its president is none other than Bishop K.H. Ting, an internationally recognized churchman and the author of many thought-provoking publications.

In May 1999, the school suspended three graduate students from the graduation ceremony. Later, it also dismissed three undergraduate students. The students wanted to sing Christian hymns instead of Communist revolutionary songs at the school's concert commemorating the

May Fourth Movement (a movement begun in 1919 to over-throw the traditional culture and usher in new thoughts, such as Communism).

The controversy, of course, went well beyond merely selecting songs. At its heart was the question of whether Christianity and socialist teaching are ideologically compatible. From the open letters below, we see dissenting voices from within the top theological school, supposedly the custodian of the official Three-Self ideology of the China Christian Council. They symbolize the theological struggle many Christians face as they search for the destiny of the Chinese church.


## The graduate students' three letters

### *An explanatory note on why we are asked to voluntarily leave the school*

On 7 May, President Ding [Bishop K.H. Ting] and Vice-President Chen asked us to leave the school voluntarily . . . [because they said] we are against the mission of the school. Bishop Ding said that this position, given on 4 May, was his personal view. Yet this view is endorsed by the government's leaders, the majority of faculty members, and some students. Therefore, it is an official position of the school . . . we have had no clear explanation of the accusations against us. There has been no chance for us to defend ourselves. In order to clarify this issue, to show our stance, we issue this letter so that teachers and students can know the truth.

The whole incident is related to the May Fourth com-memorative concert. On 26 April, the student union of the graduate students discussed the selection of songs for the concert. We suggested singing hymns for the following reasons:

1 God is the Lord of history. Christians should see God in historical events, and we should give God all the glory and praise.
2 Christian hymns can correctly express the interpretation of our faith.

Some of the classmates disagreed and suggested we could sing secular songs. They also suggested that if we sing hymns, it would cause an unfavorable impression of the graduate students ... and it may affect the future careers of some students. We debated this, with no consensus. We did not participate at that concert. We oppose politicizing this event, but someone suggested that nonparticipation in this concert is unpatriotic. This interpretation is irresponsible and distorts the facts. We believe that patriotism is not merely singing socialist songs, but effectively promoting the welfare and interests of the nation's people. Patriotism demands that we begin with our neighbors and share in their joy and suffering, and make the church an agent striving for the social good.

In fact, this incident seems related to the school's current promotion of 'pluralistic theologies' [among the traditionally evangelical and fundamentalist students]. We have made our theological stance very clear, upholding the Bible as the basis of our faith. We have also expressed our position that Jesus Christ is the head of the church and is to be unconditionally obeyed by God's people.

We do not oppose the mission of the school. We try to understand the mission of our school, as well as various school regulations, from the perspective of our faith. We are accused of being against the school's mission. However, as we examine the school mission as drafted by the Religious Affairs Bureau of the State Council, there is no requirement for us to accept the ideology, the worldview or historical view of the ruling party's beliefs. We only need accept the political leadership of the [Communist] Party and the government. This is obvious. We abide by this point.

We are called to study theology so that we can be trained to serve the society. We are willing to do our best to fulfill all the academic requirements of the school. Therefore, we reject the school's demand that we withdraw.

We ask the school to clarify this issue and to come to a fair conclusion with Christian sincerity. If it persists in its accusations against us, we demand a written statement with clear and solid evidence.

### *Why do we refuse to sing secular songs at the concert?*

Our refusal to sing secular songs has been misunderstood by many. Some people accuse us of being unpatriotic and against the school mission, which would be grounds for our dismissal. We have no choice but to clarify our stance so that people can have a clear understanding of us.

We do not oppose Christians singing secular songs, including the revolutionary songs. However, we believe that if we conduct any activity in the name of the church, we need to proclaim our faith; therefore, we have to treat it as a serious matter concerning our faith. We advance the following reasons to justify our position:

A theological school differs from a secular school. It is a fellowship of those who fully commit their life to witness to the gospel truth. It is the body of Christ. It is established to bear witness to Christ and to glorify Christ. The commemorative evening for the May Fourth Movement must bear witness to the truth that Christ is the true hope and salvation of mankind. Anything other than this motive or purpose is inappropriate.

The whole Bible describes the history of the Fall and sin of mankind. It also is a history of God's salvation and judgment. God is the true Lord of history and is the only one who should be praised in history. This is the basic position the church should hold, regardless of the context. We realize that none of the secular songs can express this truth. We believe that if we praise the achievement of mankind in the name of the church, we are self-righteous, self-deifying idol worshipers; this is inappropriate. The mission of the church is to see Christ, to proclaim the judgment of God, and to preach the message of salvation.

We believe that for true blessings to come to any country, any nation, any race, and any society, they must practice mercy and justice in obedience to God, and strive for the common good, so that all members can enjoy freedom, peace, and prosperity from God. Patriotism is any action that can promote these blessings for one's nation and people. Therefore, the church, as the body of Christ, manifests its patriotism by faithfully playing the roles of priest, prophet, and king. It should preach the gospel of truth, pray for all nations and those in power, ask for forgiveness and blessings, accuse the wicked and the unjust, and declare God's promise and hope. The church is to be servant to all in self-sacrificing humility. If the church departs from this path, it shirks its duty and brings a curse to the people and nation. We believe that if we sing these secular songs in formal assembly, we cannot fulfill our duty as the church; we may even cover up the groaning of the Holy Spirit by our hypocritical noises. To avoid our true duties, we may deceive ourselves to justify our so-called patriotic acts.

Although some may accuse us of opposing the Three-Self principle and the school's mission . . . we believe they have mistaken our position and distorted our meaning.

In fact, we follow the teaching of the Bible. We emphasize that as citizens we have to follow the law of the society, and to obey the civil authorities that have been installed by God according to his goodwill. We should obey all regulations, laws and norms. Unless the government asks us to commit crimes, we should not disobey it according to our individual will. The church, as a social organization, should follow all the laws of the government. Christians are sent into the world to follow the example of Christ, to live out the justice and mercy of the Father. We should share this burden with others while living in this world. We should work hard, serve others, promote the good of society and witness to the virtue of Christ. We live according to this principle, and we exhort Christians to do likewise.

However, we are against . . . accepting the ideology and the value system of the ruling Party. We also oppose the watering down or deleting of our faith to suit some current needs.

We feel this event did not just happen. For a long time the church has not clearly discerned its relationship with the government and society, nor has it distinguished between the teaching of the church and the dominant ideology of the country (Communism). Therefore, in some situations, it blurs the unique role and mission of the church. The sensitivity of this issue, both inside and outside of the church, suggests how critical this issue is. Today we show you the facts. We do not call for justice to be done for us. We really want to appeal to the teachers, fellow students, pastors, and coworkers to pay careful attention to this issue, especially its theological implications. We hope that you can discuss it based on the Bible and from the perspective of the church. We also hope that we can honestly proclaim and live out the teaching of Christ.

> CU SIUJI, CHEN SHUNFU, CHEN YONG
> Jinning Union Theological Seminary, Nanjing,
> 12 May 1999.

### *Mission statement of*
### *Jinning Union Theological Seminary (Nanjing)*

Our school is a Christian theological school. It trains leaders for the church in China with the following objectives:

- Politically, to support the leadership of the Chinese Communist Party;
- To love Socialist China;
- To uphold the Three-Self principle of the church in China;
- To have a certain maturity in spirituality and theological understanding;
- To have good virtue and good health;
- To be able to supply the spiritual needs of believers;
- To lead Christians into truth;
- To build the church in China in accordance with the Three-Self principle.

## Aftermath

These three students were denied their graduate diplomas. The school indicates that if, one day, the students were to retract their position, they would be able to receive their diplomas.

Meanwhile, three other students, from the undergraduate division, issued an open letter on 16 June 1999, not only expressing their dissatisfaction with how the school had treated the three graduate students, but also calling for a total break with the Three-Self principle. They say that it has been so politicized that it has lost its basic Christian character. These three students withdrew from school. Very soon, their statement became known by Christians outside of China and found its way onto the Internet. The school formally expelled them, and soon the Public Security Bureau began a nationwide search for them. They are charged with leaking state secrets and jeopardizing national security. The three remain in hiding. It is a cost many Chinese Christians must pay to uphold their convictions.

# Appendix 2

# The Case of the Lisu

Christianity, introduced to the Lisu people at the end of the nineteenth century in Burma (now called the Union of Myanmar), spread to China in the early 1920s.[1] Among the one million Lisu in the world, almost 60 percent live in Yunnan, China, concentrated in the Nujiang Canyon (formerly known as Selwin valley).[2] In spite of the unfavorable political conditions against Christianity since 1949, the Christian population among the Lisu has been growing. For example, in 1997 about 70 percent of the people in the Fugong county of Nujiang prefecture were Christian. This is the highest Christian concentration in China at the county level and the first primarily 'Christian county' in China.

Missionaries who went to Nujiang during the 1920s and 1930s were almost all from a fundamentalist background,

---

[1] Covell has written a chapter on the evangelization of the Lisu in *The Liberating Gospel in China*. See also Tien Ju-K'ang, *The Peak of Faith: Protestant Mission in Revolutionary China.* (See References section for both of these titles.)

[2] According to the Chinese government, there were 574,800 Lisu in 1995. See Jiang (1995:64).

emphasizing a dualistic worldview with strong Puritan teachings. As they encountered the Lisu, they were aware that the Lisu were very religious – they used to spend a huge amount of wealth on sacrifices to appease their gods and spirits in spite of their poverty. The traditional dowry customs made a heavy economic burden for the Lisu, who often ended up in debt. There were also many customs – such as rice wine drinking, smoking, and premarital sex – which the missionaries considered incompatible with Christianity.[3]

We shall briefly explore the social changes brought about by the missionaries that had a bearing on the Lisu Christians and their economic situation. These economic changes were praised by the Chinese government in the 1950s, despite their negative attitudes toward religion and the missionaries. The following data are drawn from the official Chinese government reports that preclude any favoritism toward Christianity.

Marriage was an expensive event for the Lisu. The groom had to pay the bride several cows for the wedding and was in debt to her family or others for many years. It was not uncommon for a family to have to sell its children into slavery in order to pay the debt. Therefore, marriage became

---

[3] As a historical record, the missionaries in Fugong used the term 'uncivilized' to describe the traditional lifestyle of the Lisu. They were, of course, trapped in their historical context, and they regarded Christianity as being a superior culture to the local ones. They also taught the Lisu Christians that a Christian lifestyle was more civilized than the traditional Lisu one. The term 'civilized' is used among Lisu Christians when they make reference to the traditional Lisu way of life. This attitude was attacked by the Chinese authorities as a form of cultural imperialism.

.a trade and was arranged by the families, instead of being decided by the bride and groom themselves. If the husband wanted a divorce, he could reclaim all he had paid. If the wife initiated a divorce, she had to pay back twice the amount she had received from her husband. Thus, a divorce led to many conflicts. Moreover, the Lisu men were allowed to have concubines, invariably causing complications in the family. Finally, all unmarried teens and adults could sleep in a 'common house' in search of sexual partners; they were allowed to engage in sexual acts freely until they got married.[4]

In 1954, a detailed study was made on the annual expenses of Lisu households. There was a well-to-do family whose son got married. The wedding cost about 38 percent of the entire household's annual net income. Immediately, the family was in debt and transformed from a well-to-do into a poor household. (Research Committee, National Minority Commission of the National People's Congress 1954:43)

The missionaries regarded these Lisu marriage customs as inappropriate and a hindrance to the spread of the gospel. Therefore, they insisted on the following teachings: Christians had to be monogamous; they were free to marry but could not divorce; premarital sex was prohibited. Since many poor young people could not afford to get married,

---

[4] On marriage customs, see Central Government Visitation Team Second Detachment Nujiang Group (1956, 1981:21–22). On the 'common house', see the Research Committee, National Minority Commission of the National People's Congress (1956:9). These 'common houses' have been abolished since the 1950s. However, such customs – premarital sexual practices – are still common and accepted among the Lisu.

the missionaries insisted that both parties forego the exchange of gifts, and the wedding feast was discouraged. Further, any consenting Christian male above the age of twenty, or female above the age of eighteen, could marry in a church free of charge.

Christians could not marry non-Christians. These new marriage customs attracted people to the church (Gao and Zhang 1990:21–22). Marriage became an institution that could be decided upon by the couple without incurring debt. There would be fewer familial disputes over divorce and concubine issues. It was thought that forced marriages, due to out-of-wedlock pregnancies arising from the 'common house', would decline. Finally, the Christian community protected marriage. As a result, many joined the church.

A Christian wedding was economically prudent for the Lisu community because of the austerity of the wedding ceremony and its related obligations. Having no wedding feast was a great help in an impoverished region and saved much food that might have been wasted.[5] The money could be used to invest in agricultural production and benefited the newlyweds.

One of the few luxuries in the harsh environment of Nujiang was alcohol consumption. Very often at the end of the first harvest, the Lisu would immediately set up a

---

[5] Kim-kwong Chan personally witnessed a Christian wedding in March 1997, and interviewed the newlyweds. Both were poor peasants who claimed that they could not afford to get married if they were not Christians and did not have the wedding in the church. Unlike most of the weddings in China, there was no feast or reception after the wedding service. Such austerity at the wedding is rather rare in China.

crude brewery in the field to make rice wine from the new grain.[6] A large quantity of grain was used to make wine and the Lisu would then lie drunk in the field for several days. Since the grain produced was often not even enough for basic consumption, frequently these households would run out of food a few months after the harvest and go into debt or live on handouts long before their second harvest. A detailed study in 1956 suggested that an average Lisu household (excluding the Christians) would use 12 to 23 percent of their annual grain production to make wine.

In addition, crops were sold for cash in order to purchase extra wine after the harvest season (Chinese Communist Party 1956:7–8). Since drinking was a must and getting drunk was culturally accepted, it would be difficult to ignore its economic significance and social consequences. Furthermore, the Lisu liked to smoke, and smoking also consumed a substantial amount of their disposable income (Central Government Visitation Team 1956:21).

The missionaries made their teachings clear on drinking alcohol and smoking: total abstinence. This was a basic requirement for all Christians, and the Christian community acted as an enforcement agency among its own. The missionaries substituted the habit of smoking with local tea drinking. It also helped those addicted to alcohol to with-

---

[6] The common drink of the Lisu is rice wine (or grain wine), which is made from a simple distillation process of the newly fermented cooked grains. The alcoholic content is between 5 and 10 percent. Technically, this type of distilled alcoholic drink is not considered hard liquor, which would have an alcoholic content of 25 to 40 percent. The Lisu also drink a form of hard liquor on special festival days, but it is produced by a special brewery and cannot be made at home or in the field.

draw from their habit. Soon the Christian families saved more money by not wasting their grain on wine making. There were fewer crimes among the Christians due to the lack of alcoholism. In the early 1950s, even the anti-religious Chinese Communist Party cadres admitted that the economic well-being of the Lisu Christians was, in general, better than that of non-Christians (Central Government Visitation Team 1956:21).

Traditional religious customs dictated that the Lisu regularly offer livestock or crops to various spirits, as well as on special occasions, such as illness and death. For example, a 1953 survey indicated that out of 37 families in Chuangmedi village of Fugong, 25 made a total of 251 sacrifices during the year. (The other families were probably Christians who made no such sacrifices.) This amounted to more than 11 percent of the total annual village income. Discounting the 12 households that made no sacrifices, the 25 households used at least 15 percent of their gross annual income or crops for such a purpose. A study of a relatively well-to-do family showed that from 1929 to 1952 they offered 16 goats, 15 chickens, and 29 pigs. Eventually, the head of the household had to sell all the land to pay the debt incurred by these offerings; he became a hired laborer whose well-being was slightly better than a slave (Chinese Communist Party 1956:7).

The Christian teaching on these sacrifices was very clear: no Christian was allowed to make any sacrifices once he or she became a believer. This was not so much for economic reasons but for theological ones: only one God was to be worshiped.

Although the missionaries instructed Christians to bring offerings to the church, the amount received did not come near the amount previously offered to spirits. The side effect of this teaching was obvious: If you became a Christian you saved money because it was less expensive to practice Christianity.[7]

The main concern of the fundamentalist missionaries was to save the lost Lisu souls from eternal damnation for worshiping the wrong god rather than to rescue them from their miserable economic predicament. Their motive was religious, but their teachings bore economic benefits. In order to teach the Lisu, the missionaries developed three basic theological teachings and the Lisu commandments (Li, Daoshing 1994:1082–1083):

1   One must be devoted to one God. One cannot believe in God and, at the same time, make offerings to other spirits.

2   God is holy. Drinking alcohol is an unholy as well as a blasphemous act. This also applies to smoking.

3   Christians are civilized; it would be uncivilized,[8] and even shameful, to accept wedding gifts from either party. Also, it would be uncivilized to waste money on a wedding feast.[9]

---

[7] As these writers interviewed Christians in the field, people said that it was cheaper to believe in Christ than traditional gods. Kim-kwong Chan had also heard similar comments in other parts of rural China in recent years.

[8] Although this is a pejorative term, the authors wish to be faithful to the facts observed in the field. This is the original term used by the missionaries and later by Lisu Christians themselves in their teachings.

[9] John and Isobel Kuhn were married in Kunming, and they did throw a big wedding party as recorded in Isobel's several writings. However, it had taken place before they went to work among the Lisu. John and Isobel did live a very austere life – a

Because these doctrinal teachings were in the form of practical guidelines, the Lisu Christians built and based their community on them. Although they sound a bit legalistic, the Lisu Christians found them easy to follow, and they helped to shape a unique community. While these teachings were never meant to be a guide for a self-sustainable economic community, one of their most obvious characteristics is the Puritan social ethic – no waste and honest work. As a result, these Christian families would eventually have a better economic situation than their non-Christian neighbors.

The Chinese government, like other restricted-access countries, does not welcome Christian mission work, but it does welcome assistance in economic development. Since the Nujiang prefecture is one of the poorest areas in all of China, the national government is targeting it for its special poverty-eradication program. Thus, the government is more open to outside help.

The Christian community is by far the strongest social unit in the Nujiang prefecture and can serve as a powerful agent to launch any social program. Although the Christian community in Fugong county is generally better off economically than its non-Christian neighbors, its members are, as a whole, still living below the poverty line. This may be attributed mainly to the increase in population

---

lifestyle that was compatible with their teachings. Not all missionaries who worked among the Lisu were like the Kuhns. The Morrisons of the Assemblies of God Church in Fugong were accused of living an extravagant life. His son was accused of raping local women, with one of them giving birth to a 'mixed-race baby'. This lady and the baby were well known in the local village; they left China for Burma in 1950. See Fu, Abu (1994:1094–1096).

(fourfold since 1950), due to better government health service since 1950, and to a special birth quota allowance given to national minorities in China.[10] At the same time, there are no funds for capital investment, technological improvement in productivity, or exploring alternative means of resource utilization.

The Christian leaders in Fugong and Nujiang are thinking of using Christian training centers and the extensive church network to promote economic development through medical and agricultural projects. Such projects, executed by committed Christians, may lead to the formation of holistic communities throughout the Nujiang prefecture.

The concept of holistic ministry parallels Food for the Hungry International's (FHI) 'Vision of a Community'. As a result of the ministry, FHI wishes to see the people of a community advance toward their God-given potential. This comes through equipping people to progress beyond meeting their basic physical needs and becoming a growing group of Christians that love God and one another, manifest the fruit of the Spirit and serve others.

Although Lisu Christian leaders have no formal theo-logical training, their theological methodology seems to be a 'from below' approach: realization of physical needs, reflection upon these needs, and pastoral action to fulfill them. At first, they taught only the Bible to their voluntary pastors, but in recent years they have realized that the needs of the Christians are physical as well as spiritual. They began

---

[10] In China, the Han Chinese can only have one single child if residing in the city and two, at the most, if they live in the countryside. However, the national minorities are not restricted by these regulations. It is a policy to protect the national minorities so that they can have a sizable community to preserve their ethnic identity.

to focus their ministry not just on spiritual teaching but also on agricultural, educational, and medical programs. They are now teaching the voluntary pastors to minister to both the spiritual and physical needs of their flocks.

Prior to World War II, the Lisu Christians began sending missionaries to evangelize their neighboring minority peoples, such as the Dulongs. The Dulongs are the most remote, the most difficult to access, and the most under-developed people group in China. It is the only minority group in China that cannot be accessed by road. Yet, among the four thousand Dulongs in Dulong valley north of Fugong, at least eight hundred are now Christians wor-shiping in seven churches,[11] all supported by the Lisu Christians. With further work, it may be possible to turn the Dulongs into a holistic Christian community through the Lisu.

Lisu Christians already have a good Christian foundation, a good testimony, a large critical mass (Fugong being a newly Christianized people with perhaps the highest rate of conversion in modern mission history), and sufficient readiness to be challenged.

The challenge before us is how best to help the Lisu build a concrete Christian community to promote the cycle of reciprocity; namely, redemption leading to development, and further, development leading to redemption. The Christian community, deeply committed to the concept of holistic ministry, will attempt to accomplish at least three general goals:

---

[11] A Lisu evangelist went to the northern part of Dulong valley in the fall of 1997 and held a series of evangelistic meetings; nearly one hundred Dulongs accepted the gospel and two new churches are being formed (Yesu, 1998). See Chapter 4.

1 Show the Chinese government that Christians can indeed make a positive contribution toward the socio-economic development of the community and the nation. The Chinese government is hospitable to Christian organizations as long as they measurably help in China's modernization effort.[12]

2 Demonstrate that the Christian community can reach out to other people groups not readily accessible to outsiders. Such outreach must be holistic in nature and able to transform the community both physically and spiritually. In other words, the cycle of reciprocity will lead the Lisu to reach out to the Dulongs by sharing the gospel and helping them to help themselves. In the end, the Dulongs will begin sharing the gospel with their neighboring, unreached people groups while helping them to help themselves.

3 Allow the Christian community to reap great dividends. Even though China is the largest populated nation in the world (1.3 billion), more than 90 percent of the Chinese are unreached. There are 55 officially recognized ethnic minority groups in China, mostly living in the rural areas.[13] Many mission models have failed to penetrate these peoples,

---

[12] The Christian church in China has raised the issue of Christianity and moral, social, intellectual and cultural modernization in recent years. However, it has not discussed economic development. See Wickeri and Cole, eds., *Christianity and Modernization: A Chinese Debate* (full details in References section).

[13] This number was established in 1956 by the State Council of the Chinese government. In fact, there are many more than 55 ethnic minority groups.

so that about half of them have not been reached by the gospel.[14] If the holistic model works among the Lisu and among the Dulongs, eventually it may become a paradigm for many other rural ethnic communities in China. Furthermore, it would be the Chinese Christians, not foreigners, who would evangelize the Chinese – a 'self-propagating' ecclesial principle that is strongly emphasized by Chinese Christian leaders.

We have seen that the emergence of Fugong into the first Christian county in China has significant implications for our missiological thinking in general, and for reaching China's unreached ethnic minorities in particular. Socialism, the state orthodoxy in China, holds a rather negative view of religion – a view based primarily on economic assumptions (that is, religion is bad for social progress and hinders economic development). In the light of this, Christians may be able to demonstrate that Christianity offers not only spiritual salvation but also economic liberation – liberating people from the yoke of poverty by applying Christian principles. The Chinese government officially closed its door to those traditional missionaries who emphasized only the other-worldly message. However, the Chinese government is open to charitable agencies that can work as equal partners with the Chinese to alleviate poverty in the rural communities, especially within the national minorities

---

[14] It also depends on the definition of 'reached'. Some ethnic minority groups, such as the Zhuang, with more than fourteen million people, have fewer than ten thousand Christians and do not have the Bible in their own languages. They are very well mixed with the Hans. Covell (1995), in his *The Liberating Gospel in China*, provides insights into this.

who inhabit the most hostile terrain in China. The Lisu Christians in Fugong are already established as a dynamic community. Can this Christian community, with resources from external Christian development agencies, establish a concrete holistic community that can act as a viable development model in China? Further, can this model be used as a missiological paradigm, opening mission frontiers in areas hitherto denied to the traditional mission approach? The story of the Lisu makes us hopeful.

# References cited in Appendix 2

Bijiang County Government, *Bijiang Xianzhi* [Bijiang County Gazeteer] (Yunnan, China: Yunnan People's Press).

Central Government Visitation Team Second Detachment Nujiang Group, 'The Religious Situation in Nujiang, 1950' in *Yunnan Minzu Oing-kuang Huijii* [Collection on Minorities Situation in Yunnan], vol. 1 (Yunnan, China: Yunnan People's Press, 1956 and 1981 [reprint]).

Chinese Communist Party, Yunnan Frontier Research Office. 'The Basic Situation of the Nujiang Lisu Autonomous Prefecture, 1956' in *Lisuzu Shihui Diaocha* [Social Survey of the Lisu Tribe] (Yunnan, China: Yunnan People's Press, 1956).

Covell, Ralph R., *The Liberating Gospel in China* (Grand Rapids, MI: Baker Book House, 1995).

Fu, Abu, 'History on the Spreading of Christianity in Fugong' in *Nujiang Wenshi Ziliao* [Collection of Historical Materials in Nujiang] (1994), 2:1094–1096.

Gao, Hanxin, and Heren Zhang, 'The Religious Issues in Nujiang' in *Nujiang Fanzhi* (Internal) (November 1990), 4 (12):20–22.

Jiang, Ling, 'A Brief Introduction to the Minority Groups in China: Lisu Nationality' in *Minzu tuanjie* [Unity of Nationality] (October 1995), 64.

Li, Daoshing, 'Survey on Christianity in Fugong', in *Nujiang Wenshi Ziliao* [Collection of Historical Materials in Nujiang] (1994), 2:1082–1083.

Research Committee, National Minority Commission of the National People's Congress, 'The Social Situation of the Lisus, 1986 reprint' in *Lisuzu Shihui Diaocha* [Social Survey of the Lisu Tribe] (Yunnan, China: Yunnan People's Press, 1956 and 1986 [reprint]).

Tien, Ju-K'ang, *The Peak of Faith: Protestant Mission in Revolutionary China* (Leiden, The Netherlands: E.J. Brill, 1993).

Wickeri, Philip L., and Lois Cole, eds, *Christianity and Modernization: A Chinese Debate* (Hong Kong: DAGA Press, 1995).

Yesu, personal correspondence in February, Gongshan Church, county seat of Gongshan county, of Nujiang Lisu autonomous prefecture of Yunnan province (1998).

The article in Appendix 2 is adapted from Tetsunao Yamamori and Kim-kwong Chan, 'Missiological Ramifications of the Social Impact of Christianity on the Lisu of China' in *Missiology* (October 1998), Vol. XXVI, No. 4, pp. 403–417. Used with permission.

# About the Authors

Tetsunao Yamamori (PhD), a native of Nagoya, Japan, is President of Food for the Hungry International and Visiting Professor in the Department of Ethnology at Central University of Nationalities, Beijing, China. He has authored, coauthored and edited numerous books. Among his books are *Penetrating Missions' Final Frontier* (InterVarsity Press, 1993), *Exploring Religious Meaning*, 5th ed. (Prentice-Hall, Inc./Simon & Schuster, 1998), and *Serving with the Urban Poor* (MARC, 1998).

Kim-kwong Chan (PhD) is Executive Secretary for Education and Training of Hong Kong Christian Council and Visiting Professor in the Department of Philosophy at Hangzhou University, China. He has authored and co-authored seven books, including *Prayers and Thoughts of Chinese Christians* (London: Mowbray, 1991) and *Protestantism in Contemporary China* (Cambridge University Press, 1993).